Coin Genesis: A Step-by-Step Guide to Creating Your Own Cryptocurrency

Table of Contents

Introduction **5**

Chapter 1 Understanding Blockchain Technology **8**

What Is Blockchain and How Does It Work? 11

Types of Blockchains: Public, Private, and Consortium 14

Consensus Mechanisms: PoW, PoS, and Beyond 16

The Role of Smart Contracts in Cryptocurrencies 19

Chapter 2 Planning Your Cryptocurrency **22**

Defining Your Coin's Purpose and Use Case 25

Choosing Between a Coin and a Token 28

Key Features and Functionalities to Consider 31

Legal and Regulatory Considerations 34

Chapter 3 Choosing a Blockchain Platform **38**

Building on an Existing Blockchain (Ethereum, Binance 41

Creating Your Own Blockchain from Scratch 43

Comparing Costs and Technical Complexities 46

Security Considerations for Blockchain Selection 49

Chapter 4 Developing the Cryptocurrency **53**

Writing the Smart Contract: Best Practices 55

Tokenomics: Supply, Distribution, and Incentives.................... 58

Gas Fees and Transaction Costs Optimization 60

Testing and Deploying Your Coin.. 63

Chapter 5 Setting Up a Blockchain Network 66

Nodes and Validators: How They Work.................................... 68

Configuring a Peer-to-Peer Network 71

Security and Encryption Protocols 73

Ensuring Decentralization and Scalability................................. 76

Chapter 6 Creating a Crypto Wallet.. 79

Types of Wallets: Hot, Cold, and Hardware Wallets 82

Generating Private and Public Keys 83

Security Best Practices for Wallet Development....................... 85

Integrating Wallets with Your Cryptocurrency 87

Chapter 7 Launching an Initial Coin Offering (ICO) or 90

ICO vs. IDO vs. IEO: Understanding the Differences 92

Creating a Whitepaper and Roadmap 96

Token Allocation and Vesting Schedules.................................. 97

Marketing Strategies for a Successful Launch 99

Chapter 8 Listing Your Coin on Exchanges............................ 103

Understanding the Exchange Listing Process.......................... 105

Centralized vs. Decentralized Exchanges (CEX vs. DEX) 108

Liquidity and Market Making Strategies....110
Compliance and KYC/AML Considerations....112
Chapter 9 Building a Crypto Community....115
Engaging with Developers and Investors....117
Social Media, Forums, and PR Strategies....120
Partnerships and Collaborations in the Crypto Space....122
Handling Community Concerns and Technical Support....125
Chapter 10 Security and Compliance....128
Common Crypto Vulnerabilities and How to Prevent Them....131
Smart Contract Auditing and Security Best Practices....134
Legal and Regulatory Compliance Across Different....137
Future-Proofing Your Cryptocurrency....140
Chapter 11 Scaling and Evolving Your Cryptocurrency....145
Upgrading the Protocol and Implementing Hard Forks....146
Cross-Chain Integrations and Interoperability....147
Staking and Yield Farming for Token Holders....148
Long-Term Sustainability and Growth Strategies....149
Conclusion....152

Introduction

Cryptocurrencies have redefined the financial landscape, challenging traditional banking systems and introducing a decentralized model of transactions that empowers individuals and businesses alike. What started with Bitcoin in 2009 as an alternative to government-issued currency has now evolved into a thriving ecosystem of digital assets, each with its unique purpose, technology, and economic model. From decentralized finance (DeFi) to tokenized assets, cryptocurrencies are no longer just a trend—they are a fundamental part of the future of money.

The idea of creating a cryptocurrency might seem complex and reserved for blockchain experts, but the truth is, with the right guidance and tools, anyone can launch their own digital currency. Whether it is for fundraising, powering a business model, facilitating transactions, or building a decentralized community, the possibilities are endless. Entrepreneurs, developers, and visionaries are recognizing the potential of custom cryptocurrencies to revolutionize industries beyond finance, including healthcare, gaming, real estate, and supply chain management.

This book is designed to serve as a practical, step-by-step guide for those looking to create their own cryptocurrency. It breaks down the technical, financial, and strategic aspects of cryptocurrency development, making it accessible to readers with varying levels of experience. You will learn the fundamentals of blockchain technology, the difference between creating a coin and a token, and the importance of choosing the right blockchain network. The book also delves into the technical components, including smart contracts, consensus mechanisms, security protocols, and transaction validation.

Beyond the technical framework, launching a cryptocurrency requires a well-thought-out strategy. Designing the economic model, setting up a governance structure, and ensuring regulatory compliance are crucial factors that influence the long-term success of any digital currency. Additionally, the book covers strategies for Initial Coin Offerings (ICOs), token sales, exchange listings, and community engagement. The role of marketing in cryptocurrency adoption cannot be overlooked, as building trust and establishing credibility in the crypto space is essential for widespread acceptance.

Security is one of the biggest concerns when launching a new cryptocurrency. The history of the crypto industry is filled with stories of hacks, frauds, and regulatory crackdowns, making it imperative to implement robust security measures from day one. The book provides insights into securing your blockchain network, conducting smart contract audits, and protecting user data to ensure your cryptocurrency is both safe and compliant.

While the potential rewards of creating a successful cryptocurrency are high, so are the risks and challenges. The crypto space is constantly evolving, and projects must adapt to technological advancements, regulatory changes, and market fluctuations. Understanding how to navigate these challenges and future-proof your cryptocurrency is a key focus of this guide.

By the end of this book, you will have the knowledge and confidence to create, launch, and manage your own cryptocurrency. Whether you are a startup founder looking to raise capital, a developer interested in blockchain innovation, or an investor exploring the crypto space, this book will serve as your blueprint. The journey from concept to a fully functional cryptocurrency requires careful planning, execution, and adaptability, but with the right approach, it can be a rewarding and transformative endeavor.

Chapter 1
Understanding Blockchain Technology

Blockchain technology has revolutionized the way we store, transfer, and verify data, introducing a decentralized, transparent, and secure method of conducting transactions across various industries. Initially developed as the underlying framework for Bitcoin, blockchain has evolved far beyond cryptocurrencies, finding applications in finance, healthcare, supply chain management, and even governance. Its ability to eliminate the need for intermediaries while ensuring data integrity has made it one of the most transformative technological advancements of the 21st century.

At its core, blockchain is a distributed ledger technology that allows information to be recorded and stored in a way that is immutable and resistant to tampering. Unlike traditional centralized databases, where a single authority controls the data, blockchain distributes its records across a network of nodes (computers), making it nearly impossible to alter past transactions. This decentralized structure enhances security, reduces fraud, and ensures transparency in all transactions.

To fully grasp the significance of blockchain technology, it is essential to understand how it works. A blockchain consists of a chain of blocks, each containing a set of transactions. Once a block is filled with data, it is verified by network participants (nodes) and then added to the chain in chronological order. Each block is secured using cryptographic hashes, making it extremely difficult to modify or delete past records. This characteristic of blockchain ensures that all transactions remain permanent and verifiable.

One of the defining features of blockchain technology is its consensus mechanism, which determines how transactions are validated and added to the blockchain. The two most common consensus mechanisms are Proof of Work (PoW) and Proof of Stake (PoS). PoW, used by Bitcoin, requires miners to solve complex mathematical puzzles to validate transactions and create new blocks. This process consumes a significant amount of computational power but ensures security and decentralization. On the other hand, PoS allows validators to create new blocks based on the number of coins they hold and are willing to "stake" as collateral. This method is considered more energy-efficient and environmentally friendly compared to PoW.

Another crucial aspect of blockchain technology is its ability to support smart contracts—self-executing contracts with predefined conditions written into code. Smart contracts automate processes, eliminating the need for intermediaries in various transactions. For example, in supply chain management, smart contracts can be used to automatically release payments once goods are delivered and verified, reducing the risk of fraud and delays. Similarly, in the financial sector, smart contracts enable decentralized lending and borrowing without the need for traditional banks.

Blockchain technology is categorized into three main types: public, private, and consortium blockchains. Public blockchains, such as Bitcoin and Ethereum, are open to anyone and operate on a decentralized network of nodes. These blockchains prioritize security and transparency but often face scalability issues due to high transaction volumes. Private blockchains, on the other hand, are controlled by a single organization or entity, making them more scalable and efficient but less decentralized. Consortium blockchains represent a hybrid approach, where multiple organizations share control over the network while maintaining a degree of decentralization.

Despite its numerous advantages, blockchain technology is not without challenges. Scalability remains a significant issue, as networks like Bitcoin and Ethereum struggle with slow transaction speeds and high fees during periods of heavy usage. Various solutions, such as the Lightning Network and Ethereum 2.0, are being developed to address these limitations. Additionally, regulatory uncertainty poses a challenge for widespread blockchain adoption, as governments and financial institutions grapple with how to integrate decentralized systems within existing legal frameworks.

Security is another critical consideration in blockchain technology. While the blockchain itself is highly secure due to its cryptographic nature, vulnerabilities can arise in applications built on top of it. Hacks and exploits targeting smart contracts, crypto wallets, and exchanges have resulted in significant financial losses over the years. Ensuring robust security measures, such as regular code audits and multi-factor authentication, is essential for maintaining trust in blockchain systems.

Beyond finance, blockchain is being explored for a wide range of applications. In healthcare, blockchain can be used to securely store and share patient records, ensuring data privacy and reducing medical errors. In voting systems, blockchain has the potential to enhance election transparency by providing a tamper-proof digital voting ledger. The supply chain industry is also benefiting from blockchain's ability to track products from origin to destination, improving transparency and reducing fraud.

The future of blockchain technology is filled with promise, as ongoing research and innovation continue to expand its capabilities. With advancements in scalability, security, and interoperability, blockchain has the potential to become the backbone of a new digital economy. Whether in cryptocurrencies, decentralized finance, or beyond, understanding blockchain technology is crucial for anyone looking to navigate the rapidly evolving digital landscape.

This chapter will explore the fundamental principles of blockchain technology, providing a clear understanding of its mechanisms, types, and applications. By the end of this chapter, you will have a strong grasp of how blockchain works, its benefits and challenges, and its potential to reshape industries worldwide.

What Is Blockchain and How Does It Work?

Blockchain is a groundbreaking technology that has transformed the way data is stored, shared, and secured. Initially introduced as the underlying framework for Bitcoin, blockchain has evolved into a powerful system with applications far beyond cryptocurrencies. It is a decentralized, distributed ledger that records transactions across multiple computers in a network. This ensures that data remains immutable, transparent, and secure, making blockchain one of the most significant innovations in modern technology.

At its core, blockchain consists of a chain of blocks, each containing a list of transactions. These transactions are verified by multiple network participants before being permanently added to the chain. Unlike traditional databases, where a central authority has control, blockchain operates through a peer-to-peer network, eliminating the need for intermediaries. Each block is secured using cryptographic hashing, ensuring that once data is recorded, it cannot be altered or deleted. This immutability makes blockchain highly resistant to fraud, hacking, and unauthorized modifications.

The process of blockchain transaction verification relies on a consensus mechanism, a set of rules that determine how new transactions are validated. The most widely used consensus mechanisms are Proof of Work (PoW) and Proof of Stake (PoS). PoW, employed by Bitcoin, requires participants to solve complex mathematical puzzles to validate transactions and create new blocks. This process, known as mining, consumes a significant amount of computational power but ensures network security. PoS, used by networks like Ethereum 2.0, selects validators based on the number of tokens they hold and are willing to stake as collateral. PoS is considered more energy-efficient than PoW, reducing the environmental impact associated with blockchain operations.

Blockchain transactions follow a systematic process to ensure security and integrity. When a user initiates a transaction, it is broadcast to the network, where it is verified by nodes—computers that participate in maintaining the blockchain. Once verified, the transaction is grouped with others into a block. Each block contains a unique cryptographic hash that links it to the previous block, forming an unbreakable chain. This linking process ensures that any attempt to alter a previous block would require recalculating all subsequent hashes, an almost impossible task due to the computational effort required.

One of blockchain's most revolutionary aspects is its ability to remove the need for intermediaries. Traditional financial transactions often involve banks, payment processors, and third-party services, adding complexity, time, and costs. Blockchain enables direct peer-to-peer transactions, allowing users to transfer digital assets instantly and securely without relying on centralized institutions. This has opened the door to decentralized finance (DeFi), where financial services such as lending, borrowing, and trading occur without traditional banks.

Beyond finance, blockchain has found applications in various industries. In supply chain management, blockchain enhances transparency by tracking products from origin to delivery, reducing fraud and ensuring authenticity. In healthcare, blockchain secures patient records, preventing data breaches while allowing seamless access to medical history. Governments are exploring blockchain for secure voting systems, ensuring tamper-proof elections. The technology is also revolutionizing real estate, intellectual property rights, and identity verification by providing a trusted, decentralized record of ownership.

Security is a defining feature of blockchain technology. Each transaction is encrypted, and the decentralized nature of the system makes it nearly impossible for a single entity to manipulate data. However, vulnerabilities can arise in applications built on blockchain, such as smart contracts and cryptocurrency exchanges. Hacks and exploits targeting weak security measures have resulted in significant financial losses. To mitigate these risks, blockchain developers implement rigorous security audits, multi-signature authentication, and decentralized storage solutions.

Despite its benefits, blockchain faces challenges that hinder widespread adoption. Scalability remains a major concern, as popular networks like Bitcoin and Ethereum struggle with slow transaction speeds and high fees during periods of congestion. Efforts to improve scalability include second-layer solutions like the Lightning Network and Ethereum's transition to PoS. Additionally, regulatory uncertainty presents a challenge, as governments and financial institutions navigate the legal implications of decentralized digital assets.

The future of blockchain is promising, with ongoing advancements aimed at enhancing efficiency, security, and interoperability between different blockchain networks. As businesses and individuals continue to explore blockchain's potential, the technology is expected to become an integral part of digital finance, supply chain logistics, data security, and beyond. Understanding how blockchain works is essential for anyone looking to harness its capabilities and participate in the digital revolution.

Types of Blockchains: Public, Private, and Consortium

Blockchain technology comes in different types, each designed to meet specific needs and use cases. The three main categories of blockchains are public, private, and consortium blockchains. These variations differ in terms of accessibility, control, security, and governance, allowing businesses and organizations to choose a model that aligns with their requirements.

Public blockchains are the most decentralized and open form of blockchain networks. Anyone can join, participate, and validate transactions without needing permission from a central authority. These blockchains operate on a peer-to-peer network, where all transactions are recorded on a distributed ledger accessible to everyone. Public blockchains rely on consensus mechanisms such as Proof of Work (PoW) or Proof of Stake (PoS) to validate transactions and secure the network. Bitcoin and Ethereum are prime examples of public blockchains, enabling users to conduct transactions transparently without relying on banks or intermediaries. The main advantage of public blockchains is their security and transparency, as all participants can verify transactions independently. However, they face challenges related to scalability, slower transaction speeds, and high energy consumption due to the intensive computational work required for consensus.

Private blockchains, also known as permissioned blockchains, restrict access to a specific group of participants. Unlike public blockchains, where anyone can participate, private blockchains are controlled by a single organization or a governing entity that decides who can read, write, and validate transactions. This model is commonly used by businesses and enterprises that require data confidentiality and greater transaction efficiency. Private blockchains offer faster transaction processing and greater scalability compared to public blockchains, as fewer nodes are involved in reaching consensus. They are commonly used in supply chain management, finance, and healthcare, where data privacy is crucial. While private blockchains provide enhanced control and efficiency, they are less decentralized and may face trust issues since a central authority governs the network.

Consortium blockchains, also known as federated blockchains, represent a hybrid model that combines elements of both public and private blockchains. Instead of being controlled by a single entity, a consortium blockchain is managed by a group of organizations or institutions that collectively maintain the network. This type of blockchain is ideal for industries that require collaboration among multiple stakeholders, such as banking, healthcare, and trade finance. In a consortium blockchain, selected participants are granted permission to validate transactions and maintain the ledger, ensuring a balance between decentralization and control. These blockchains provide improved scalability, privacy, and efficiency compared to public blockchains while reducing the centralization risks of private blockchains. However, setting up and maintaining a consortium blockchain requires coordination among multiple parties, which can lead to governance challenges.

Each type of blockchain serves a distinct purpose, catering to different levels of transparency, security, and accessibility. Public blockchains are best suited for applications requiring full decentralization and trustless interactions, such as cryptocurrencies and decentralized finance (DeFi). Private blockchains are ideal for enterprises that prioritize data security and fast transactions, such as supply chain tracking and corporate record-keeping. Consortium blockchains offer a balanced approach, allowing multiple organizations to collaborate securely while maintaining controlled access. As blockchain technology continues to evolve, businesses and developers must carefully evaluate their needs to choose the right type of blockchain for their projects. Understanding these variations ensures that blockchain applications align with the intended goals while optimizing efficiency, security, and governance.

Consensus Mechanisms: PoW, PoS, and Beyond

Consensus mechanisms are fundamental to blockchain technology, as they determine how transactions are validated and new blocks are added to the chain. A consensus mechanism ensures that all participants in a blockchain network agree on the current state of the ledger without requiring a central authority. Different blockchains use different consensus mechanisms to achieve security, decentralization, and efficiency. The most common consensus models include Proof of Work (PoW) and Proof of Stake (PoS), but newer mechanisms are also emerging to address the limitations of traditional models.

Proof of Work (PoW) is the original consensus mechanism, first introduced with Bitcoin. In PoW, miners compete to solve complex mathematical puzzles using computational power. The first miner to find the correct solution gets the right to add a new block to the blockchain and is rewarded with cryptocurrency. This process, known as mining, ensures network security by making it computationally expensive and time-consuming to alter past transactions. While PoW is highly secure and decentralized, it has significant drawbacks, including high energy consumption, slow transaction speeds, and expensive mining hardware requirements. Networks like Bitcoin and Ethereum (before its transition to PoS) have faced scalability issues due to PoW's resource-intensive nature.

Proof of Stake (PoS) was developed as an alternative to PoW, aiming to improve energy efficiency and transaction speed. In a PoS system, validators are chosen to create new blocks based on the number of coins they hold and are willing to "stake" as collateral. Instead of solving mathematical puzzles, validators are incentivized to act honestly since they risk losing their staked coins if they attempt fraudulent activities. PoS reduces the need for massive computational power, making it more environmentally friendly and scalable than PoW. Ethereum transitioned to PoS with its Ethereum 2.0 upgrade to enhance efficiency and sustainability. However, one concern with PoS is that it can lead to wealth concentration, as those with more tokens have greater control over block validation.

Beyond PoW and PoS, several innovative consensus mechanisms have been developed to improve blockchain performance and address scalability, security, and decentralization concerns.

Delegated Proof of Stake (DPoS) is a variation of PoS in which token holders vote for a small group of delegates who validate transactions on their behalf. This model is faster and more efficient than traditional PoS but introduces a level of centralization. Projects like EOS and TRON use DPoS to process transactions more quickly while maintaining network integrity.

Proof of Authority (PoA) is another alternative where block validation is performed by a limited number of approved validators, typically organizations or trusted entities. PoA is highly efficient and scalable, making it suitable for enterprise blockchains. However, it sacrifices decentralization, as trust is placed in a select group of validators rather than a distributed network of participants.

Proof of History (PoH), used by Solana, introduces a novel approach by timestamping transactions before they are included in the blockchain. This method significantly increases transaction speed and efficiency, allowing networks to process thousands of transactions per second. PoH is particularly beneficial for high-speed decentralized applications but requires a different trust model than traditional PoW or PoS.

Hybrid consensus models combine elements of multiple mechanisms to optimize performance. Some blockchains integrate PoW with PoS or other mechanisms to balance security, efficiency, and decentralization. For example, Ethereum's transition from PoW to PoS has been part of a larger effort to create a more sustainable yet secure network.

Consensus mechanisms are at the heart of blockchain innovation, influencing security, scalability, and usability. While PoW remains a gold standard for security, PoS and newer models have gained traction due to their efficiency and lower environmental impact. As blockchain technology continues to evolve, consensus mechanisms will play a critical role in shaping the future of decentralized systems, ensuring they remain secure, efficient, and scalable for global adoption.

The Role of Smart Contracts in Cryptocurrencies

Smart contracts play a crucial role in the functionality and evolution of cryptocurrencies, enabling decentralized automation and trustless execution of agreements without intermediaries. A smart contract is a self-executing contract in which the terms and conditions are written in code and automatically executed when predefined conditions are met. These contracts run on blockchain networks, ensuring transparency, security, and immutability. By eliminating the need for third-party intermediaries such as banks, lawyers, or notaries, smart contracts reduce transaction costs, increase efficiency, and minimize the risk of fraud.

The foundation of smart contracts was laid by Ethereum, which introduced the concept as a core feature of its blockchain. While Bitcoin's blockchain primarily supports peer-to-peer transactions, Ethereum extended blockchain functionality to enable decentralized applications (dApps) and automated contract execution. Smart contracts are written in programming languages like Solidity and are deployed onto the Ethereum Virtual Machine (EVM), where they interact with digital assets, execute transactions, and enforce agreements without human intervention.

One of the primary use cases of smart contracts in cryptocurrencies is facilitating decentralized finance (DeFi). DeFi applications leverage smart contracts to provide financial services such as lending, borrowing, trading, and yield farming without relying on traditional financial institutions. For example, lending platforms like Aave and Compound use smart contracts to automatically manage loans, ensuring borrowers meet collateral requirements and lenders receive interest payments. This automation increases efficiency and removes barriers to accessing financial services, especially for unbanked populations.

Smart contracts also play a significant role in Initial Coin Offerings (ICOs) and tokenization. When launching a new cryptocurrency, developers use smart contracts to create and distribute tokens according to predefined rules. This ensures fair distribution and compliance with the project's whitepaper. Similarly, security token offerings (STOs) and non-fungible tokens (NFTs) utilize smart contracts to manage ownership rights, royalties, and transfers of digital assets.

The security and trustlessness of smart contracts are among their most valuable attributes. Once deployed on the blockchain, smart contracts cannot be altered, ensuring that agreements are executed exactly as programmed. This immutability prevents tampering and enhances trust among participants. Additionally, transactions executed through smart contracts are recorded on the blockchain, providing a transparent and verifiable audit trail.

Despite their advantages, smart contracts are not without challenges. One major concern is code vulnerabilities. If a smart contract is poorly written or contains bugs, it can be exploited by hackers, leading to significant financial losses. High-profile incidents such as the DAO hack in 2016, where attackers exploited a vulnerability in an Ethereum smart contract to drain millions of dollars, highlight the importance of thorough security audits and best practices in smart contract development.

Another challenge is legal and regulatory uncertainty. Since smart contracts operate autonomously and are not governed by traditional contract laws, disputes can arise when unexpected issues occur. Governments and regulatory bodies are still exploring ways to integrate smart contracts into legal frameworks while preserving the benefits of decentralization.

As blockchain technology advances, smart contracts are expected to become more sophisticated, with improvements in security, interoperability, and efficiency. New blockchain platforms, such as Polkadot, Cardano, and Solana, are enhancing smart contract capabilities by offering faster transaction speeds, lower costs, and better scalability than Ethereum. Additionally, Layer-2 solutions and off-chain computation methods aim to optimize smart contract performance without compromising security.

Smart contracts are a cornerstone of cryptocurrency ecosystems, enabling automation, efficiency, and decentralization. Their applications extend beyond finance into supply chain management, healthcare, real estate, and governance, demonstrating their potential to revolutionize multiple industries. As the technology continues to evolve, smart contracts will play an even greater role in shaping the future of decentralized systems and digital economies.

Chapter 2
Planning Your Cryptocurrency

Ceating a cryptocurrency is more than just writing code and launching a token—it requires a well-thought-out plan that considers its purpose, utility, and long-term sustainability. With thousands of cryptocurrencies in the market, only a fraction achieve widespread adoption and real-world utility. To ensure success, careful planning is essential from the very beginning. This chapter focuses on the fundamental aspects of planning a cryptocurrency, including defining its purpose, selecting the right blockchain model, understanding tokenomics, and addressing legal and regulatory challenges.

The first and most important step in planning a cryptocurrency is identifying its purpose and value proposition. Every successful cryptocurrency has a well-defined objective that distinguishes it from others. Bitcoin was created as a decentralized alternative to traditional currencies, Ethereum introduced smart contract functionality, and stablecoins were designed to provide price stability in a volatile crypto market. Before developing a cryptocurrency, creators must ask themselves: What problem does it solve? Who is the target audience? How will it provide value to users? Without a clear purpose, a cryptocurrency risks becoming another speculative asset with no long-term viability.

Another crucial decision is choosing between creating a coin or a token. A coin operates on its own independent blockchain, such as Bitcoin or Ethereum, and requires significant development effort, including building a consensus mechanism, securing the network, and maintaining nodes. On the other hand, a token is built on an existing blockchain like Ethereum, Binance Smart Chain, or Solana, allowing for easier deployment and integration with decentralized applications (dApps). Tokens can serve various purposes, such as utility tokens used within ecosystems, governance tokens that provide voting rights, or security tokens representing assets.

The tokenomics of a cryptocurrency—how it is structured economically—is another vital element in the planning phase. Tokenomics determines the supply, distribution, incentives, and overall financial model that drives user adoption and network growth. Decisions such as whether to have a fixed supply (like Bitcoin's 21 million cap) or an inflationary model, how tokens will be allocated (e.g., to developers, investors, or users), and what mechanisms will encourage demand (staking, burning, rewards) significantly impact the cryptocurrency's long-term success. Poorly designed tokenomics can lead to issues like price instability, lack of adoption, or network centralization.

Security is another critical factor to consider in the planning phase. Cryptocurrencies, due to their digital and decentralized nature, are often targeted by hackers. Planning must include strategies for securing the network against threats such as 51% attacks, smart contract vulnerabilities, and phishing scams. If the cryptocurrency involves smart contracts, thorough code audits should be performed to prevent exploits. Developers must also decide whether the cryptocurrency will use a Proof of Work (PoW), Proof of Stake (PoS), or another consensus mechanism, as each has different security implications and operational requirements.

Regulatory and legal compliance cannot be ignored when planning a cryptocurrency. Governments worldwide are establishing regulations to govern digital assets, and failing to comply can lead to legal consequences or restrictions on trading. Some jurisdictions require Know Your Customer (KYC) and Anti-Money Laundering (AML) measures, while others impose restrictions on token sales and Initial Coin Offerings (ICOs). Developers and entrepreneurs must research and understand the regulatory environment in the countries where they plan to launch their cryptocurrency to avoid potential legal hurdles.

Building a strong community and ecosystem is also essential during the planning phase. A cryptocurrency without an engaged user base has little chance of success. Community-driven projects often gain significant traction because users feel involved in the decision-making process. Strategies such as airdrops, staking rewards, developer grants, and strategic partnerships can help grow the network. Additionally, planning for exchange listings, liquidity provisions, and market-making strategies will ensure the cryptocurrency is accessible for trading and adoption.

Another consideration is the long-term roadmap and scalability. Many cryptocurrencies struggle with scalability issues as user adoption increases. Planning should include solutions such as Layer 2 scaling, interoperability with other blockchains, and on-chain governance mechanisms to ensure sustainability. A well-defined roadmap helps investors and users understand the project's vision and future goals, building trust in the development team.

Creating a cryptocurrency requires more than technical expertise—it requires strategic planning across multiple dimensions, from economic design and security to regulation and community building. Without careful preparation, even the most innovative projects can fail due to poor execution or lack of adoption. This chapter provides a comprehensive guide on how to strategically plan a cryptocurrency, ensuring that it stands out in a competitive and rapidly evolving market.

Defining Your Coin's Purpose and Use Case

Before launching a cryptocurrency, one of the most critical steps is defining its purpose and use case. The success of a cryptocurrency depends on its ability to solve a real problem, provide value to users, and sustain long-term adoption. Without a clear purpose, a cryptocurrency risks becoming just another speculative asset with no real-world utility. In a highly competitive market filled with thousands of digital currencies, having a well-defined objective is what sets a project apart.

The first question every cryptocurrency creator must ask is: What problem does this coin solve? Bitcoin, for example, was created to provide a decentralized alternative to traditional financial systems, eliminating the need for banks and intermediaries. Ethereum introduced smart contracts, enabling developers to build decentralized applications (dApps) on its blockchain. Similarly, stablecoins were designed to address the volatility of cryptocurrencies by pegging their value to traditional fiat currencies like the U.S. dollar. Without a clear problem-solving focus, a cryptocurrency may struggle to attract users and investors.

Another key factor in defining a cryptocurrency's purpose is understanding its target audience. Is the coin meant for everyday transactions like Bitcoin Cash or Litecoin? Is it designed for businesses to facilitate international payments, as Ripple (XRP) does? Will it be used within a specific industry, such as healthcare, supply chain management, or gaming? Defining the target audience helps shape the coin's functionality, marketing strategy, and overall adoption plan. A cryptocurrency designed for financial inclusion, for example, should focus on fast, low-cost transactions to serve unbanked populations effectively.

Once the purpose is established, the next step is to define the use case. A coin's use case refers to how it will function in the ecosystem and what unique value it offers. There are several common use cases for cryptocurrencies, including:

- Medium of Exchange: Cryptocurrencies like Bitcoin, Litecoin, and Dash are primarily used for transactions, allowing people to buy goods and services without relying on traditional payment systems.
- Store of Value: Some cryptocurrencies, such as Bitcoin, are seen as digital gold, holding value over time and acting as a hedge against inflation.
- Utility Tokens: Many cryptocurrencies power decentralized applications, granting users access to specific features, such as governance, staking, or premium services. Ethereum's ETH and Binance Coin (BNB) fall into this category.
- Security Tokens: These represent ownership in a company or asset and must comply with financial regulations. They are used in asset tokenization, where real-world assets like real estate or stocks are represented on the blockchain.

- Stablecoins: Coins like USDT, USDC, and DAI maintain a stable value by being pegged to fiat currencies, commodities, or algorithmic stabilization mechanisms.
- Governance Tokens: In decentralized projects, governance tokens give holders voting power in decision-making, shaping the future of the network. Examples include Uniswap (UNI) and MakerDAO (MKR).

Understanding the use case also means determining how the coin will interact with other blockchain applications. Will it be used exclusively within a single ecosystem, or will it have interoperability with multiple blockchains? The success of a cryptocurrency often depends on its ability to integrate with existing decentralized finance (DeFi) platforms, non-fungible tokens (NFTs), and other emerging blockchain innovations.

Token distribution and economic incentives play a vital role in defining a cryptocurrency's purpose. How will new tokens be issued? Will they be mined, staked, or distributed through an Initial Coin Offering (ICO)? If the coin is designed to encourage user participation, staking rewards or yield farming may be implemented to incentivize network security and liquidity. A strong tokenomics model ensures long-term sustainability, preventing problems such as inflation, centralization, or rapid price crashes.

Security and scalability must also be considered when defining a coin's purpose. If a cryptocurrency is intended for high-speed transactions, then choosing a blockchain that supports fast processing times and low fees is essential. Many new projects focus on improving blockchain scalability, with solutions such as Layer 2 networks, sharding, and sidechains. Ensuring that a cryptocurrency can handle increasing demand without sacrificing security or decentralization is crucial for long-term success.

Finally, legal and regulatory considerations must align with the coin's purpose. If a cryptocurrency is intended for financial transactions, compliance with Know Your Customer (KYC) and Anti-Money Laundering (AML) regulations may be necessary. Security tokens must adhere to financial laws governing securities, while stablecoins must comply with banking regulations. Ignoring regulatory requirements can lead to legal challenges, making it harder for the cryptocurrency to gain mainstream adoption.

Defining a cryptocurrency's purpose and use case is the foundation for its development and adoption. Without a clear objective, strong economic incentives, and real-world utility, even the most technologically advanced cryptocurrency may fail to gain traction. By identifying the problem it solves, targeting the right audience, ensuring seamless integration with blockchain ecosystems, and maintaining legal compliance, a cryptocurrency can position itself for long-term growth and success in the digital economy.

Choosing Between a Coin and a Token

When planning a cryptocurrency, one of the most fundamental decisions is whether to create a coin or a token. While both serve as digital assets on a blockchain, they have distinct characteristics, use cases, and technical requirements. Understanding the differences between coins and tokens is crucial for determining the best approach for a project, as each has its own advantages and limitations.

A coin operates on its own independent blockchain. Examples of coins include Bitcoin (BTC), Ethereum (ETH), and Binance Coin (BNB). These cryptocurrencies serve as the primary currency for their respective blockchains, meaning that transactions and applications are processed directly on their network. Creating a coin requires developing an entirely new blockchain infrastructure, which includes setting up nodes, designing a consensus mechanism, and ensuring network security. This approach provides greater control and flexibility, but it also demands extensive development expertise, resources, and ongoing maintenance.

Coins are typically used as a store of value, a medium of exchange, or to facilitate transactions on a native blockchain. Bitcoin, for instance, was designed as a decentralized alternative to traditional money, allowing users to transfer value without intermediaries. Ethereum, on the other hand, is not only a currency but also powers the execution of smart contracts and decentralized applications (dApps). Some blockchain platforms create their own coins to incentivize network participation, such as mining rewards in Proof of Work (PoW) systems or staking rewards in Proof of Stake (PoS) models.

On the other hand, a token is built on an existing blockchain, such as Ethereum, Binance Smart Chain, or Solana. Instead of having its own network, a token relies on the infrastructure of the host blockchain for security, validation, and transaction processing. This makes it easier, faster, and more cost-effective to create a token compared to developing a coin from scratch. Tokens are commonly used in Initial Coin Offerings (ICOs), decentralized finance (DeFi), gaming, and non-fungible tokens (NFTs).

There are different types of tokens based on their functionality. Utility tokens grant users access to services or products within a blockchain ecosystem. For example, Basic Attention Token (BAT) is used in the Brave browser for rewarding content creators and users. Security tokens represent ownership in an asset, such as company shares or real estate, and must comply with financial regulations. Stablecoins, such as USDT and USDC, are pegged to fiat currencies and designed to maintain price stability. Governance tokens provide holders with voting rights to influence the development and policies of a decentralized protocol, such as Uniswap's UNI token.

The choice between a coin and a token depends on the purpose of the cryptocurrency and the level of control needed. If the goal is to build a fully independent blockchain with unique functionalities, a coin is the better option. However, if the primary aim is to launch a digital asset quickly for use in a specific ecosystem, creating a token is more practical. Tokens benefit from the security and infrastructure of established blockchains, reducing the complexity of network maintenance and upgrades.

Another key consideration is scalability and adoption. Launching a new blockchain requires attracting users, developers, and miners or validators to maintain the network. Many projects fail due to a lack of adoption and liquidity. Tokens, by contrast, can be easily integrated with existing DeFi platforms, decentralized exchanges (DEXs), and smart contracts, giving them immediate utility.

Regulatory compliance is also an important factor. Creating an independent coin means taking full responsibility for regulatory approvals, network security, and governance. Tokens, especially those issued on established blockchains, often benefit from the existing legal frameworks of their host networks, making compliance easier.

In summary, choosing between a coin and a token depends on the project's technical requirements, use case, scalability, security, and regulatory considerations. Coins offer greater autonomy and control but require significant resources for development and maintenance. Tokens, on the other hand, provide a cost-effective and efficient way to launch a cryptocurrency, leveraging the security and infrastructure of existing blockchains. By carefully evaluating these factors, developers and entrepreneurs can determine the best approach for their cryptocurrency project.

Key Features and Functionalities to Consider

When creating a cryptocurrency, the features and functionalities of the digital asset determine its usability, security, and adoption. A well-designed cryptocurrency must have a strong technological foundation, economic model, and user-friendly integration to succeed in the competitive crypto market. From transaction speed to smart contract capabilities, every feature plays a role in ensuring the efficiency and scalability of the project. Here are the key elements that must be considered when developing a cryptocurrency.

One of the most fundamental aspects is transaction speed and scalability. The ability of a blockchain to process transactions quickly and efficiently determines how well it can handle real-world use cases. Bitcoin, for example, has relatively slow transaction speeds due to its Proof of Work (PoW) consensus mechanism, while newer blockchains like Solana and Binance Smart Chain focus on high throughput and low fees. Developers must choose between scalability solutions like Layer-2 protocols, sidechains, or sharding to enhance transaction speed without compromising decentralization or security.

Consensus mechanism is another critical component that affects how transactions are validated and secured on the network. Proof of Work (PoW) relies on miners solving complex cryptographic puzzles, offering strong security but consuming significant energy. Proof of Stake (PoS) allows validators to secure the network based on the number of coins they hold, reducing energy consumption while maintaining security. Other models like Delegated Proof of Stake (DPoS), Proof of Authority (PoA), and hybrid systems offer various trade-offs between decentralization, efficiency, and security. Selecting the right consensus mechanism depends on the cryptocurrency's intended use case and technical goals.

Security is one of the most important considerations when designing a cryptocurrency. Blockchain networks must be resistant to 51% attacks, smart contract vulnerabilities, and other cyber threats. Implementing encryption standards, multi-signature wallets, and smart contract auditing can help mitigate risks. Additionally, security measures such as anti-money laundering (AML) compliance and Know Your Customer (KYC) protocols may be required to meet regulatory standards, especially for financial and enterprise-focused cryptocurrencies.

Smart contract functionality is essential for cryptocurrencies that aim to power decentralized applications (dApps) and automated transactions. Smart contracts allow developers to build self-executing agreements that trigger specific actions when conditions are met. Platforms like Ethereum, Binance Smart Chain, and Polkadot support smart contract execution, enabling applications such as decentralized finance (DeFi), non-fungible tokens (NFTs), and decentralized exchanges (DEXs). If a cryptocurrency aims to support a broader ecosystem, smart contract compatibility must be a core feature.

Tokenomics and governance also play a significant role in a cryptocurrency's long-term sustainability. The economic design of a cryptocurrency includes factors such as total supply, distribution mechanisms, staking incentives, and transaction fees. A well-structured tokenomics model ensures network security, user participation, and fair value distribution. Some projects incorporate deflationary mechanisms such as token burning, while others reward users through staking and liquidity mining.

Privacy and anonymity are additional features that influence the adoption of a cryptocurrency. While most blockchains provide transparency, some projects prioritize anonymity by implementing privacy-focused features like zero-knowledge proofs (ZKPs), ring signatures, and stealth addresses. Monero and Zcash are examples of privacy coins that allow users to conduct confidential transactions without exposing wallet balances or identities.

Interoperability is becoming increasingly important as blockchain ecosystems grow. A successful cryptocurrency should have the capability to interact with other blockchain networks, facilitating cross-chain transactions and integration with multiple platforms. Technologies such as bridges, wrapped tokens, and interoperable protocols (like Polkadot and Cosmos) allow cryptocurrencies to connect with other blockchain networks, increasing their utility and adoption.

Another crucial factor is governance mechanisms, which determine how decisions are made within a blockchain network. Some cryptocurrencies adopt on-chain governance, where token holders vote on protocol upgrades and changes, while others rely on off-chain governance structures involving developers and foundation teams. Decentralized Autonomous Organizations (DAOs) have emerged as a popular governance model, enabling community-driven decision-making through token-based voting systems.

Finally, user accessibility and integration must be considered when designing a cryptocurrency. The ease with which users can buy, store, and use the digital asset influences adoption rates. Wallet support, exchange listings, and mobile-friendly applications enhance accessibility. A strong developer ecosystem with clear documentation, SDKs (Software Development Kits), and APIs (Application Programming Interfaces) can also drive innovation by encouraging third-party development and integration.

Creating a cryptocurrency requires a balanced approach, ensuring that the right combination of security, efficiency, scalability, and usability is built into the project. Whether the goal is to power a decentralized financial system, enable smart contracts, or facilitate private transactions, selecting the right features and functionalities is critical for success. A well-planned cryptocurrency that addresses these key considerations can achieve widespread adoption and long-term sustainability in the evolving digital economy.

Legal and Regulatory Considerations

Launching a cryptocurrency involves navigating complex legal and regulatory landscapes. Governments worldwide are working to establish clear guidelines for digital assets, and compliance is critical to ensuring long-term sustainability. Regulatory challenges vary by jurisdiction, and failure to comply with applicable laws can result in penalties, restrictions, or even the shutdown of a project. Understanding legal considerations helps cryptocurrency developers and entrepreneurs avoid legal pitfalls, gain investor trust, and ensure the legitimacy of their projects.

One of the first regulatory considerations is the classification of the cryptocurrency. Different jurisdictions categorize cryptocurrencies as securities, commodities, payment instruments, or utility tokens, depending on their function. For example, the U.S. Securities and Exchange Commission (SEC) applies the Howey Test to determine if a digital asset qualifies as a security. If a cryptocurrency is classified as a security, it must comply with securities laws, including registration, investor disclosures, and compliance measures. Projects that fail to meet these requirements may face enforcement actions, as seen in cases against ICOs (Initial Coin Offerings) that did not follow proper regulatory protocols.

Another crucial factor is Know Your Customer (KYC) and Anti-Money Laundering (AML) compliance. Many countries require cryptocurrency exchanges and service providers to implement KYC procedures, verifying user identities to prevent fraud, money laundering, and terrorist financing. AML regulations ensure that funds are not used for illicit activities, requiring companies to monitor transactions and report suspicious activity. Compliance with these regulations is especially critical for projects that involve token sales, crypto exchanges, or DeFi platforms.

Taxation policies are another major consideration. Governments are increasingly treating cryptocurrencies as taxable assets, requiring individuals and businesses to report their holdings, gains, and transactions. Some countries impose capital gains taxes on cryptocurrency trades, while others classify crypto as property or income. Projects must establish clear tax guidelines for their users, particularly in regions where non-compliance can lead to significant penalties.

Regulatory authorities also focus on data privacy and security laws. Many jurisdictions have enacted strict privacy regulations, such as the General Data Protection Regulation (GDPR) in Europe, which governs how personal data is collected, stored, and used. Projects that collect user data, such as crypto exchanges and wallet providers, must ensure compliance with these laws to protect user privacy and avoid fines.

In addition to financial regulations, intellectual property (IP) laws can affect cryptocurrency projects. Developers must be cautious when using existing blockchain technologies, as some blockchain patents and proprietary algorithms are protected under IP laws. Creating a unique codebase or licensing existing blockchain solutions legally can prevent infringement claims and legal disputes.

Another growing area of concern is decentralized finance (DeFi) regulation. DeFi platforms operate without intermediaries, offering lending, borrowing, and trading services through smart contracts. Regulators are increasingly scrutinizing DeFi projects to ensure consumer protection and financial stability. Some jurisdictions require DeFi projects to register as financial service providers or comply with bank-like regulations, such as ensuring proper risk management and financial disclosures.

Cryptocurrency projects must also consider stablecoin regulations, as governments and central banks are tightening oversight on digital assets pegged to fiat currencies. Regulatory concerns around stablecoins involve reserve backing, financial disclosures, and systemic risks. Some regulators require issuers to maintain full reserves, undergo audits, and ensure consumer protection measures are in place.

Legal frameworks for cross-border transactions and international compliance are another challenge. Cryptocurrencies operate on a global scale, but regulations differ from country to country. A project compliant in one jurisdiction may face restrictions in another. For example, China has banned cryptocurrency trading, while countries like Switzerland and Singapore have established favorable regulations for blockchain businesses. Projects must assess international regulations to determine where they can legally operate.

The evolving landscape of Central Bank Digital Currencies (CBDCs) also influences crypto regulations. Governments exploring CBDCs may introduce new laws affecting the use of decentralized cryptocurrencies. Some countries may impose stricter controls on digital assets to maintain monetary stability, while others may integrate crypto-friendly policies alongside their CBDCs.

To mitigate regulatory risks, cryptocurrency projects should engage legal advisors and regulatory experts early in the development process. Legal compliance should be built into the project's foundation, ensuring adherence to securities laws, taxation rules, and data protection requirements. Conducting regulatory risk assessments and consulting with financial authorities can help projects operate legally and gain legitimacy.

Understanding and adhering to legal and regulatory requirements is essential for any cryptocurrency initiative. Navigating compliance challenges ensures the project's credibility, fosters investor confidence, and enables long-term growth in a rapidly changing regulatory environment. As governments continue to refine digital asset regulations, staying informed and proactive in legal matters will be key to building a successful and legally compliant cryptocurrency.

Chapter 3 Choosing a Blockchain Platform

Selecting the right blockchain platform is a critical decision when creating a cryptocurrency. The choice of blockchain affects security, scalability, transaction speed, smart contract capabilities, and the overall functionality of the digital asset. With numerous blockchain platforms available, each offering distinct features, developers and entrepreneurs must carefully evaluate their project's needs before making a decision.

The first consideration is whether to build a new blockchain from scratch or use an existing blockchain. Creating an independent blockchain provides full control over the network's design, security protocols, and governance structure. This approach is ideal for projects that require unique functionalities, high customizability, or enterprise-level solutions. However, developing a new blockchain demands significant technical expertise, time, and resources. It also requires building a network of validators or miners to maintain security and decentralization, which can be a major challenge for new projects.

For most cryptocurrency projects, using an existing blockchain is the preferred option. Established blockchain platforms offer robust security, scalability solutions, and built-in smart contract functionality, reducing the need for extensive development efforts. Projects can launch tokens on these blockchains quickly, benefiting from existing infrastructure, developer communities, and network effects.

Ethereum is the most widely used blockchain for cryptocurrency projects, primarily due to its smart contract capabilities and extensive developer ecosystem. It supports ERC-20 tokens for fungible assets and ERC-721/1155 for non-fungible tokens (NFTs). Ethereum's shift from Proof of Work (PoW) to Proof of Stake (PoS) through Ethereum 2.0 has improved its scalability and energy efficiency. However, Ethereum still faces challenges related to high gas fees and network congestion, prompting some projects to seek alternative platforms.

Binance Smart Chain (BSC) is another popular choice, offering lower transaction fees and faster processing times than Ethereum. BSC is compatible with the Ethereum Virtual Machine (EVM), allowing developers to deploy Ethereum-based applications with minimal modifications. However, BSC operates with fewer validators, making it more centralized than Ethereum, which may be a concern for projects that prioritize decentralization.

For projects focused on high-speed transactions and low fees, Solana has gained significant traction. Solana uses a unique Proof of History (PoH) consensus mechanism, enabling it to process thousands of transactions per second. Its architecture is optimized for scalability, making it an attractive choice for DeFi applications, NFT projects, and gaming platforms. Despite its advantages, Solana has experienced network outages, raising concerns about its reliability under high transaction loads.

Polkadot and Cosmos are blockchain platforms designed for interoperability and cross-chain compatibility. Polkadot uses parachains to enable multiple blockchains to operate in parallel while maintaining security through its central Relay Chain. Cosmos employs the Inter-Blockchain Communication (IBC) protocol to facilitate seamless interaction between different blockchain networks. These platforms are ideal for projects requiring cross-chain transactions or specialized blockchain customization.

For enterprises and private blockchain applications, Hyperledger and Corda provide permissioned blockchain solutions with advanced security and regulatory compliance. Unlike public blockchains, permissioned blockchains restrict participation to authorized entities, making them suitable for businesses that need privacy and controlled access.

Security is another crucial factor in choosing a blockchain platform. Established networks like Ethereum and Bitcoin have proven resilience against attacks, while newer blockchains may still be undergoing security testing. Smart contract vulnerabilities are a common risk, so platforms with strong security audit frameworks and developer support should be prioritized.

Scalability plays a major role in ensuring long-term viability. Some blockchains, like Ethereum, rely on Layer-2 scaling solutions such as Polygon to improve transaction throughput and reduce fees. Projects must assess whether the chosen blockchain can handle expected transaction volumes as user adoption grows.

Regulatory considerations also impact the choice of blockchain. Some platforms, like Ripple (XRP), are designed for compliance with financial regulations, making them suitable for institutional adoption. Other blockchains, particularly those with privacy-focused features like Monero, may face stricter regulatory scrutiny.

Choosing the right blockchain platform requires balancing factors such as scalability, security, decentralization, transaction costs, smart contract capabilities, and regulatory compliance. Projects that prioritize ease of deployment and ecosystem support often choose Ethereum or Binance Smart Chain, while those needing custom solutions may opt for Polkadot, Cosmos, or Solana. Understanding these factors ensures that the selected blockchain aligns with the project's goals, providing a solid foundation for long-term success.

Building on an Existing Blockchain (Ethereum, Binance Smart Chain, Solana)

When creating a cryptocurrency or decentralized application (dApp), using an existing blockchain is often the most practical and efficient approach. Instead of building a blockchain from scratch, developers can leverage the security, infrastructure, and community of established networks like Ethereum, Binance Smart Chain (BSC), and Solana. Each of these blockchains offers unique advantages and trade-offs, making the choice dependent on factors such as transaction speed, cost, smart contract capabilities, and scalability.

Ethereum is the most widely used blockchain for smart contracts and token creation, supporting thousands of decentralized applications, DeFi projects, and NFTs. Launched in 2015, Ethereum pioneered the concept of smart contracts, enabling developers to create programmable assets and automate transactions without intermediaries. Ethereum supports various token standards, including ERC-20 (fungible tokens) and ERC-721/1155 (NFTs), making it the preferred choice for launching new tokens.

However, Ethereum has faced significant challenges related to high gas fees and network congestion. The network operates on a Proof of Stake (PoS) model after transitioning from Proof of Work (PoW) with Ethereum 2.0, improving energy efficiency and transaction speeds. Despite this, gas fees can still be costly during peak usage, making it less ideal for projects that require frequent microtransactions. To mitigate these issues, developers often integrate Layer-2 scaling solutions like Polygon to improve transaction efficiency.

Binance Smart Chain (BSC) was developed as a faster and more cost-effective alternative to Ethereum. It is EVM-compatible, meaning developers can deploy Ethereum-based smart contracts on BSC with minimal modifications. BSC offers lower transaction fees and faster block times compared to Ethereum, making it attractive for DeFi projects and token launches.

BSC uses a Proof of Staked Authority (PoSA) consensus mechanism, which allows for quick transaction processing but comes at the cost of decentralization. The network is controlled by a limited number of validators, primarily selected by Binance, making it more centralized than Ethereum. Despite this, BSC has gained widespread adoption due to its affordability and ease of use, particularly for projects focused on DeFi, gaming, and tokenized assets.

Solana is known for its high-speed and low-cost transactions, making it a popular choice for developers who require scalability and efficiency. Unlike Ethereum and BSC, which rely on traditional blockchain validation mechanisms, Solana uses a unique Proof of History (PoH) system combined with Proof of Stake (PoS) to achieve high throughput. This allows Solana to process thousands of transactions per second (TPS) with fees significantly lower than Ethereum.

Solana is particularly attractive for NFTs, gaming, and high-frequency DeFi applications where speed is crucial. However, the network has experienced occasional outages and security concerns, leading some developers to question its long-term stability. Despite these issues, Solana remains a top choice for projects prioritizing transaction efficiency.

When choosing between Ethereum, Binance Smart Chain, and Solana, developers must consider their project's specific requirements. Ethereum is best for projects that need strong decentralization, network security, and widespread adoption. Binance Smart Chain offers an affordable and easy-to-use environment with fast transactions but is more centralized. Solana provides high-speed performance and low fees but has faced network reliability issues.

Developers must also consider developer tools, community support, and ecosystem integration when selecting a blockchain. Ethereum has the largest developer ecosystem and extensive documentation, while BSC offers seamless integration with Binance products. Solana, though newer, has gained rapid adoption and support from Web3 projects.

Ultimately, the choice of blockchain depends on factors such as cost, speed, scalability, decentralization, and ecosystem compatibility. By leveraging existing blockchain infrastructure, developers can focus on building innovative applications while avoiding the complexities of maintaining their own blockchain network.

Creating Your Own Blockchain from Scratch

Building a blockchain from scratch is a complex but rewarding process that offers complete control over the network's architecture, security mechanisms, governance model, and tokenomics. Unlike launching a token on an existing blockchain like Ethereum or Binance Smart Chain, creating a new blockchain allows for customization tailored to specific use cases such as finance, supply chain management, gaming, or decentralized applications. However, developing a blockchain requires significant technical expertise, infrastructure, and long-term maintenance.

The first step in creating a blockchain is defining its purpose and functionality. A blockchain can be designed for different applications, such as digital payments, smart contracts, decentralized finance (DeFi), or enterprise solutions. For example, Bitcoin was built as a decentralized digital currency, while Ethereum introduced a platform for smart contracts and dApps. Clearly identifying the blockchain's objectives will guide decisions on its consensus mechanism, scalability solutions, and governance structure.

One of the most critical aspects of blockchain development is choosing a consensus mechanism, which determines how transactions are validated and added to the blockchain. The most common mechanisms include:

- Proof of Work (PoW): Used by Bitcoin, PoW requires miners to solve complex mathematical problems to validate transactions. It is highly secure but consumes significant energy and can be slow.
- Proof of Stake (PoS): Validators are selected based on the number of coins they hold and are willing to stake as collateral. PoS is energy-efficient and provides faster transactions.
- Delegated Proof of Stake (DPoS): Token holders vote for a set number of validators who process transactions on their behalf, improving scalability while maintaining decentralization.

- Proof of Authority (PoA): A small group of approved validators maintains the blockchain, making it efficient but more centralized.
- Hybrid Models: Some blockchains combine multiple consensus mechanisms to optimize security, speed, and decentralization.

Once the consensus mechanism is chosen, the next step is developing the blockchain's architecture. This includes designing the following core components:

1. Node Infrastructure: Nodes store copies of the blockchain, validate transactions, and maintain network security. Deciding between a fully decentralized, semi-decentralized, or centralized node structure is crucial.
2. Block Structure: Blocks contain transaction data, a timestamp, a cryptographic hash, and a reference to the previous block. The size and frequency of block creation impact performance.
3. Smart Contract Capability: If the blockchain will support dApps, it must have a built-in virtual machine (e.g., Ethereum's EVM) and a programming language like Solidity or Rust.

4. Native Cryptocurrency: A new blockchain typically has its own native currency, used for transaction fees, staking, or governance. The total supply, distribution model, and economic incentives must be defined.

Security is a primary concern when building a blockchain. The network must implement cryptographic encryption, private and public keys, and decentralized validation to prevent fraud and attacks. Measures such as 51% attack resistance, DDoS protection, and transaction finality mechanisms are essential for maintaining network integrity.

Scalability solutions must also be considered, especially if the blockchain aims to support high transaction volumes. Layer-2 solutions, sharding, sidechains, and off-chain computation can improve performance without compromising decentralization.

After designing the architecture, the next phase is developing the blockchain protocol. This involves writing the source code using programming languages such as C++, Python, Go, or Rust. Open-source blockchain frameworks like Hyperledger Fabric, Tendermint, or Substrate can accelerate development. The blockchain must undergo rigorous testing and debugging to identify security vulnerabilities and performance issues.

Once the blockchain is functional, the launch process includes deploying the genesis block (the first block of the chain), setting up nodes, and establishing network governance. A successful launch requires thorough documentation, developer support, and community engagement.

Creating a blockchain from scratch offers maximum customization and independence but requires ongoing maintenance, security updates, and infrastructure costs. Only projects with strong technical expertise and a clear use case should consider building an independent blockchain. By carefully planning and executing each step, developers can create a robust and scalable blockchain tailored to their vision and objectives.

Comparing Costs and Technical Complexities

When deciding whether to create a new blockchain or use an existing one, it is essential to consider the costs and technical complexities involved. Each approach presents its own set of challenges, financial requirements, and development efforts that must align with the goals and resources of the project. Building a blockchain from scratch requires significant investment in infrastructure, security, and ongoing maintenance, while using an established blockchain reduces costs but comes with certain limitations.

Developing a new blockchain involves creating an independent network with a unique consensus mechanism, smart contract capabilities, and governance structure. This requires hiring blockchain developers, security experts, and DevOps engineers, making it an expensive and time-consuming process. The cost of building a fully functional blockchain can range from hundreds of thousands to millions of dollars, depending on the complexity of the network. Infrastructure costs also play a significant role, as maintaining a decentralized network requires nodes, validators, and continuous software updates. Additionally, security is a major concern, as newly developed blockchains are more vulnerable to cyberattacks, requiring robust encryption protocols, resistance against 51% attacks, and extensive auditing. Without proper security measures, the blockchain could be exploited, leading to financial losses and loss of trust from users.

On the other hand, creating a token on an existing blockchain is a much more cost-effective and efficient alternative. Platforms like Ethereum, Binance Smart Chain, and Solana provide ready-made infrastructure, allowing projects to launch quickly without developing a blockchain from scratch. The cost of creating a token on an established network is significantly lower, as it only involves smart contract deployment and token distribution, eliminating the need for independent nodes and network maintenance. Additionally, existing blockchains offer built-in security and scalability solutions, ensuring that projects benefit from well-established consensus mechanisms and high transaction throughput. However, using an existing blockchain comes with trade-offs, such as dependency on network conditions, potential congestion issues, and the need to comply with the blockchain's standards and fee structures.

Scalability is another crucial factor when comparing the two approaches. A newly developed blockchain allows for complete control over transaction speed, block size, and consensus mechanisms, but achieving high throughput requires significant optimization. This can involve implementing sharding, Layer-2 scaling solutions, or alternative validation methods, all of which increase development complexity and costs. Existing blockchains, on the other hand, already have scalability features in place, such as Ethereum's Layer-2 solutions and Solana's high-speed processing capabilities. These platforms enable projects to scale without extensive development efforts, reducing technical barriers for adoption.

Regulatory and compliance costs also differ between the two options. A new blockchain must establish its own compliance framework, ensuring adherence to legal requirements, Know Your Customer (KYC) procedures, Anti-Money Laundering (AML) regulations, and securities laws. This often requires engaging legal experts, conducting jurisdictional research, and obtaining regulatory approvals, leading to additional expenses. Token projects on existing blockchains benefit from well-defined regulatory frameworks, making it easier to navigate legal challenges. However, they must still comply with token sale regulations, taxation policies, and security classifications, which can add to operational costs.

Time to market is another critical factor in the decision-making process. Developing a new blockchain from scratch can take several months to years, as it requires coding, rigorous testing, security audits, and community building before launching. The need for extensive debugging, optimization, and network stability testing further extends the timeline. In contrast, launching a token on an existing blockchain can be completed within weeks or months, as smart contract templates and predefined standards simplify the development process. The ability to quickly enter the market gives token-based projects a competitive advantage, particularly in fast-moving sectors like decentralized finance (DeFi) and non-fungible tokens (NFTs).

Ultimately, the choice between building a new blockchain and using an existing one depends on the project's objectives, budget, technical capabilities, and long-term vision. If the goal is to create a highly customized, independent blockchain with unique features, then investing in a proprietary network may be justified despite the high costs and complexities. However, if the primary focus is on launching a functional cryptocurrency with minimal development overhead, leveraging an existing blockchain offers a more practical and cost-effective solution. Careful evaluation of these factors will ensure that the chosen approach aligns with the project's strategic goals while optimizing resources and reducing risks.

Security Considerations for Blockchain Selection

Security is one of the most critical factors when selecting a blockchain platform for cryptocurrency development. A secure blockchain ensures the integrity, confidentiality, and availability of transactions while protecting against cyber threats, fraud, and network attacks. Different blockchains offer varying levels of security, depending on their consensus mechanisms, decentralization models, and built-in security protocols. Understanding these factors is essential for making an informed decision about which blockchain to use.

The consensus mechanism of a blockchain plays a fundamental role in its security. Proof of Work (PoW), used by Bitcoin, provides high security due to the immense computational power required to manipulate transactions. However, PoW blockchains are vulnerable to 51% attacks, where a single entity controlling the majority of mining power could alter transaction history or double-spend funds. Proof of Stake (PoS) and its variations, such as Delegated Proof of Stake (DPoS) and Proof of Authority (PoA), offer more energy-efficient alternatives with different security trade-offs. PoS systems rely on validators who stake their tokens as collateral, making attacks financially impractical but still susceptible to governance manipulation if a small group of validators gains excessive control.

Decentralization is another major security factor. A blockchain with a large and distributed network of nodes is more resistant to attacks than a centralized or semi-centralized system. Public blockchains like Ethereum and Bitcoin have thousands of nodes, making it nearly impossible for a single entity to alter the ledger. In contrast, private or consortium blockchains, which are controlled by a limited number of participants, offer faster processing speeds but introduce trust concerns, as a small group of validators can manipulate transactions. Projects must assess whether they prioritize decentralization for security or centralized control for efficiency.

Network security also depends on encryption protocols and cryptographic hash functions. Most blockchains use SHA-256 or Keccak hashing algorithms to secure transactions and ensure data integrity. However, the rise of quantum computing presents potential future threats to these encryption methods. Some blockchains are developing quantum-resistant cryptographic algorithms to safeguard against this risk. Ensuring a blockchain is built with advanced cryptographic standards reduces vulnerabilities to emerging threats.

Smart contract security is another key consideration, especially for projects planning to use Ethereum, Binance Smart Chain, or Solana. Smart contracts are self-executing programs that automate transactions, but if they contain vulnerabilities, they can be exploited by hackers. High-profile attacks, such as the DAO hack on Ethereum in 2016, resulted in millions of dollars in losses due to smart contract flaws. To mitigate risks, developers should conduct smart contract audits, use standardized contract libraries, and implement secure coding practices. Platforms like Ethereum have extensive resources for smart contract development, while newer blockchains may require additional scrutiny to ensure security.

Blockchain scalability also affects security. Networks experiencing high congestion, like Ethereum during peak usage, can become slow and expensive to use, leading users to seek alternative platforms. However, choosing a blockchain with low transaction fees and fast processing times must be balanced with security trade-offs. Some high-speed blockchains achieve efficiency by reducing decentralization, making them more vulnerable to attacks. Solutions like Layer-2 scaling, sharding, and sidechains improve performance while maintaining security.

Regulatory compliance and security frameworks are essential for projects that require adherence to legal standards. Some blockchains, like Ripple and Hyperledger, are designed with built-in compliance features, making them suitable for financial institutions and enterprises. Ensuring a blockchain has support for KYC (Know Your Customer), AML (Anti-Money Laundering), and data privacy laws like GDPR can prevent legal issues and enhance security for users.

Another important factor is the blockchain's security track record. Some blockchains have faced repeated outages or vulnerabilities, raising concerns about their reliability. Examining past incidents, developer response times, and community support can help determine whether a blockchain is secure enough for long-term use. Blockchains with active developer communities, frequent updates, and strong governance mechanisms are generally more resilient to threats.

Ultimately, selecting a blockchain with strong security features requires a careful evaluation of consensus mechanisms, decentralization, cryptographic standards, smart contract security, scalability, regulatory compliance, and historical security performance. Projects that prioritize security can avoid costly breaches, maintain user trust, and ensure long-term sustainability in the evolving blockchain ecosystem.

Chapter 4
Developing the Cryptocurrency

Developing a cryptocurrency is a complex process that requires careful planning, technical expertise, and strategic decision-making. Whether creating a standalone blockchain or launching a token on an existing platform, the development process involves several crucial steps, including coding, security implementation, testing, and deployment. Each stage must be executed with precision to ensure a functional, secure, and scalable cryptocurrency that meets the needs of its intended users.

The first step in cryptocurrency development is defining the underlying blockchain or token standard. If building a new blockchain, developers must design its architecture, consensus mechanism, and governance model. This requires selecting between Proof of Work (PoW), Proof of Stake (PoS), or hybrid consensus models, each of which impacts security, scalability, and decentralization. On the other hand, if launching a token, the choice of blockchain platform (Ethereum, Binance Smart Chain, Solana, or others) is critical, as it determines transaction speed, network fees, and compatibility with decentralized applications.

Once the blockchain or token standard is chosen, the next step is writing the source code. This involves developing the core functionality, such as transaction validation, block creation, smart contracts, and security protocols. Programming languages vary depending on the blockchain—Ethereum-based tokens use Solidity, while standalone blockchains may use C++, Rust, or Python. Smart contract development requires special attention, as vulnerabilities in contract logic can lead to exploits, hacks, or loss of funds. To mitigate risks, developers use standardized contract libraries and conduct thorough security audits before deployment.

Security is a top priority in cryptocurrency development. Implementing encryption protocols, digital signatures, and private key management ensures that transactions are secure and resistant to fraud. To prevent 51% attacks and double-spending issues, the network must have a strong node infrastructure and distributed consensus model. For token-based cryptocurrencies, security measures such as multi-signature wallets, transaction limits, and automated contract verification help protect against exploits.

Once the core code is developed, extensive testing is required. Developers conduct unit tests, integration tests, and stress tests to identify bugs, optimize performance, and ensure transaction integrity. Testnet environments allow developers to simulate real-world conditions before launching on the mainnet. Public beta testing can also help gather community feedback and identify potential security risks.

After testing, the cryptocurrency is deployed on its respective network. If launching a new blockchain, this involves setting up genesis nodes, distributing initial coins, and ensuring network stability. If deploying a token, smart contracts must be deployed on the chosen blockchain, with proper verification and liquidity provision for decentralized exchange listings.

Post-launch, maintaining and updating the cryptocurrency is an ongoing process. Developers must monitor network performance, implement software upgrades, and respond to security threats. Governance mechanisms, such as decentralized autonomous organizations (DAOs), can enable community-driven decisions on protocol upgrades and feature implementations.

A well-developed cryptocurrency balances security, scalability, and usability. Whether it functions as a medium of exchange, a governance token, or a utility asset, careful development ensures its success in a competitive market. By following best practices in coding, security, testing, and deployment, developers can create a robust and sustainable cryptocurrency that meets user needs while adapting to the evolving blockchain landscape.

Writing the Smart Contract: Best Practices

Writing a smart contract is a crucial step in cryptocurrency development, as it defines how transactions, token distribution, and automated processes function within the blockchain ecosystem. Smart contracts are self-executing programs stored on the blockchain, ensuring trustless and transparent interactions without intermediaries. However, poor coding practices can lead to security vulnerabilities, hacks, and financial losses. Following best practices in smart contract development helps minimize risks and ensures a reliable and efficient cryptocurrency.

The first consideration in smart contract development is choosing the right blockchain platform and programming language. Ethereum is the most widely used blockchain for smart contracts, with Solidity as its primary programming language. Other platforms, such as Binance Smart Chain (BSC) and Solana, offer similar functionality but use different languages like Rust or Move. Selecting the appropriate blockchain depends on factors like transaction fees, scalability, and ecosystem compatibility.

Security is the most critical aspect of writing a smart contract. Exploitable vulnerabilities, such as reentrancy attacks, integer overflows, and logic flaws, can result in significant losses. One of the most infamous examples is the DAO hack on Ethereum, where a flaw in a smart contract allowed an attacker to drain millions of dollars. To mitigate security risks, developers should follow secure coding practices, including implementing reentrancy guards, using safe math libraries, and avoiding unnecessary complexity in contract logic.

Code simplicity and efficiency enhance both security and performance. A well-structured smart contract should have minimal redundancy, clear function definitions, and optimized gas consumption. Gas fees, which users pay to execute smart contract functions, can become costly if contracts are inefficient. Developers can reduce gas costs by optimizing storage variables, avoiding unnecessary state changes, and using efficient looping structures. Tools like Solidity's optimizer and gas estimation features help refine contract efficiency.

Thorough testing is essential before deploying a smart contract to the blockchain. Unit tests, integration tests, and simulated stress tests help identify potential bugs and security loopholes. Testnets, such as Ethereum's Rinkeby and Binance's Testnet, allow developers to deploy and test contracts in a controlled environment before launching on the mainnet. Automated testing frameworks like Hardhat and Truffle provide tools for debugging and ensuring contract reliability.

Smart contract audits add an extra layer of security. External security firms specialize in auditing contracts to detect vulnerabilities and suggest fixes. While audits can be expensive, they are necessary for projects handling significant financial transactions or token ecosystems. Well-audited smart contracts enhance investor confidence and reduce the risk of exploits.

Proper access control mechanisms prevent unauthorized modifications or exploitations. Using role-based permissions ensures that only authorized accounts can execute administrative functions. Implementing functions such as Ownable contracts, multi-signature authentication, and time-locked upgrades can protect against malicious activities.

Transparent and well-documented code improves maintainability and trust. Including comments, clear function names, and structured documentation allows developers and community members to understand the contract's logic and functionality. Open-source projects often benefit from community contributions and audits, strengthening security and innovation.

Upgradability is another key consideration when designing smart contracts. Since blockchain transactions are immutable, upgrading a deployed contract can be challenging. Using proxy contract patterns, such as the OpenZeppelin Transparent Proxy, enables future upgrades without disrupting the contract's existing state or functionality. However, upgrade mechanisms must be designed carefully to balance flexibility with security.

Once a smart contract is finalized, deployment must be handled with caution. Ensuring the correct parameters, verifying the contract on blockchain explorers, and monitoring initial transactions help prevent deployment errors. Smart contract ownership should be carefully managed to avoid centralized risks, such as a single entity having excessive control over contract functions.

By following best practices in smart contract development, developers can create secure, efficient, and scalable blockchain applications. Strong security measures, optimized gas usage, comprehensive testing, and transparent documentation contribute to the long-term success of a cryptocurrency project. As blockchain technology continues to evolve, adhering to best practices ensures that smart contracts remain robust, adaptable, and resistant to emerging threats.

Tokenomics: Supply, Distribution, and Incentives

Tokenomics, a combination of "token" and "economics," refers to the economic model that governs a cryptocurrency's supply, distribution, and incentives. A well-designed tokenomics structure is critical for the success and sustainability of a blockchain project, as it influences adoption, price stability, and long-term viability. When designing a cryptocurrency, developers must carefully plan its supply mechanisms, distribution strategy, and incentives to align with the project's goals and ecosystem growth.

One of the foundational aspects of tokenomics is supply management, which determines how many tokens will exist and how they will be created or removed from circulation. Cryptocurrencies typically have either a fixed supply or an inflationary supply. A fixed supply, like Bitcoin's 21 million cap, creates scarcity and can drive value appreciation over time. Inflationary models, used in networks like Ethereum, continuously generate new tokens to incentivize validators and sustain network operations. Some projects implement controlled inflation or deflation mechanisms, such as token burning, to regulate supply and maintain balance between demand and availability.

Distribution plays a crucial role in ensuring fair access to the token and preventing excessive centralization. Tokens can be distributed through several methods, including pre-mining, initial coin offerings (ICOs), airdrops, staking rewards, and liquidity mining. Pre-mining involves allocating a portion of tokens to the founding team, early investors, and developers before public release. ICOs allow projects to raise funds by selling tokens to investors before the official launch. Airdrops distribute free tokens to users as a marketing strategy, while staking and liquidity mining reward users for securing the network or providing liquidity to decentralized exchanges.

Incentive structures are key to encouraging user participation and network security. Many blockchain projects use staking mechanisms to reward users who lock their tokens to validate transactions and maintain the blockchain. Yield farming and liquidity mining provide incentives for users to supply liquidity to decentralized finance (DeFi) platforms. Governance tokens enable holders to participate in decision-making processes, giving them a stake in the project's future direction. Properly designed incentives attract users, increase adoption, and create a self-sustaining ecosystem.

Token utility is another important aspect of tokenomics, defining how the token is used within the ecosystem. Some tokens serve as a medium of exchange, allowing users to buy goods and services. Others provide access to specific features, such as governance, staking, or premium services. Utility tokens like Ethereum's ETH are required to pay transaction fees, while Binance Coin (BNB) is used for discounted trading fees on Binance's platform. The more use cases a token has, the greater its demand and long-term sustainability.

Security and stability mechanisms must also be considered when designing tokenomics. Vesting schedules prevent early investors and team members from dumping large amounts of tokens immediately after launch, reducing price volatility. Lock-up periods ensure that funds allocated for development, partnerships, and marketing remain committed to the project's long-term growth. Some projects introduce algorithmic mechanisms to stabilize token value, such as supply adjustments based on market demand.

A well-structured tokenomics model fosters trust and confidence in the cryptocurrency, encouraging participation from investors, developers, and users. By balancing supply dynamics, fair distribution, and strong incentives, blockchain projects can create a thriving ecosystem with sustained growth. Thoughtful tokenomics design not only enhances adoption but also strengthens the overall economic viability of the cryptocurrency, ensuring long-term success in the competitive digital asset market.

Gas Fees and Transaction Costs Optimization

Gas fees and transaction costs play a significant role in blockchain usability, affecting both user experience and the viability of decentralized applications (dApps). Gas fees are the charges required to execute transactions or smart contract operations on a blockchain network, compensating miners or validators for their computational work. High transaction costs can limit adoption, reduce efficiency, and make certain blockchain use cases, such as microtransactions and decentralized finance (DeFi), less practical. Optimizing gas fees and transaction costs is essential for improving blockchain performance and increasing user participation.

One of the primary factors influencing gas fees is network congestion. When blockchain networks experience high demand, transaction fees surge as users compete to have their transactions processed quickly. Ethereum, for example, has faced periods of excessive gas fees due to congestion, making transactions costly for users. To address this, developers can implement Layer-2 scaling solutions such as rollups, sidechains, and state channels. Rollups, like Optimistic Rollups and zk-Rollups, batch multiple transactions into a single transaction before submitting it to the main blockchain, significantly reducing costs. Sidechains, such as Polygon, provide alternative networks where transactions can be processed at lower fees while still benefiting from Ethereum's security.

Another way to optimize transaction costs is through efficient smart contract design. Poorly optimized smart contracts consume excessive computational resources, leading to high gas fees. Developers can minimize costs by reducing redundant computations, optimizing storage usage, and using gas-efficient data structures. Solidity, the primary programming language for Ethereum smart contracts, offers best practices for optimizing code execution, such as using calldata instead of memory storage and avoiding unnecessary state changes. Pre-auditing and testing contracts in simulated environments can help detect inefficiencies before deployment.

Gas fee optimization also depends on choosing the right blockchain for specific use cases. Some networks are designed to offer lower transaction costs and higher throughput compared to Ethereum. Binance Smart Chain (BSC), Solana, and Avalanche provide cost-effective alternatives, making them attractive for projects that require frequent transactions. Solana, for instance, uses a unique Proof of History (PoH) mechanism, allowing it to process thousands of transactions per second at minimal fees. However, choosing an alternative blockchain comes with trade-offs, such as potential centralization risks and ecosystem compatibility.

Dynamic gas fee models also help optimize costs. Ethereum's London Hard Fork introduced the EIP-1559 upgrade, which replaced the traditional auction-based fee model with a base fee and priority tip system. This upgrade improved fee predictability and reduced unnecessary fee spikes. Other blockchains implement flexible fee structures, adjusting transaction costs based on network conditions and demand. Users can also benefit from gas price estimation tools that recommend optimal transaction fees based on current network activity.

For blockchain projects, integrating gasless transactions can improve user experience. Meta-transactions allow third parties, such as dApp developers, to cover gas fees on behalf of users, enabling seamless onboarding and increasing accessibility. Some DeFi platforms implement transaction fee subsidies or token-based fee discounts to encourage usage while reducing cost barriers.

Batching transactions is another effective method for reducing costs. Instead of processing multiple individual transactions, developers can combine multiple operations into a single blockchain interaction. This reduces the number of on-chain transactions, lowering gas fees while improving efficiency. Projects that involve high-frequency trading, NFT minting, or DeFi interactions can significantly benefit from transaction batching.

By implementing Layer-2 solutions, optimizing smart contract efficiency, selecting cost-effective blockchains, leveraging dynamic fee models, and utilizing meta-transactions, developers and users can reduce gas fees and transaction costs. As blockchain technology continues to evolve, further innovations in scalability and fee optimization will enhance blockchain accessibility, making decentralized applications more practical for mainstream adoption.

Testing and Deploying Your Coin

Testing and deploying a cryptocurrency is a crucial phase in development, ensuring that the blockchain or token operates securely, efficiently, and as intended. Without rigorous testing, vulnerabilities, inefficiencies, and bugs can compromise the integrity of the project, leading to financial losses or security breaches. A well-planned deployment strategy minimizes risks and provides a smooth transition from development to live usage.

The first step in testing a cryptocurrency is unit testing, which focuses on individual components of the blockchain or smart contract. Developers must verify that transaction functions, consensus mechanisms, and cryptographic security measures work as expected. For token-based cryptocurrencies, smart contract functionalities such as token transfers, approvals, staking, and governance mechanisms need thorough validation. Tools like Truffle, Hardhat, and Foundry help automate testing for Ethereum-based tokens, while blockchain-specific testing frameworks exist for other networks.

After unit testing, integration testing ensures that different components of the blockchain or token interact correctly. This includes testing wallet compatibility, transaction validation across nodes, and network synchronization. If the cryptocurrency involves smart contracts, integration testing verifies that external dependencies, such as oracles and decentralized applications (dApps), function properly. Developers should simulate various network conditions, including congestion, latency, and potential attack scenarios.

Security testing is one of the most critical phases. Smart contract audits help detect vulnerabilities like reentrancy attacks, integer overflows, and unauthorized access. Independent security firms or blockchain audit platforms such as CertiK, OpenZeppelin, and Trail of Bits conduct comprehensive code reviews to ensure robustness. Bug bounty programs can further enhance security by incentivizing ethical hackers to identify flaws before deployment.

Once internal testing is complete, the cryptocurrency is deployed on a testnet, a simulated blockchain environment that mirrors real-world conditions without financial risk. Testnets allow developers and users to interact with the cryptocurrency in a sandbox environment, verifying transaction execution, gas fees, and contract functionality. Ethereum offers multiple testnets, including Sepolia and Goerli, while Binance Smart Chain (BSC) and Solana have their own dedicated testnets. Testing on multiple networks helps identify potential issues before moving to the mainnet.

After successful testnet trials, mainnet deployment takes place. For independent blockchains, this involves setting up genesis blocks, bootstrapping validator nodes, and configuring network parameters. If launching a token, developers must deploy the smart contract to the chosen blockchain, ensuring that contract verification is completed on blockchain explorers like Etherscan or BscScan. Proper access control should be implemented to prevent unauthorized modifications post-deployment.

Post-deployment monitoring is essential for identifying issues early. Real-time analytics, log tracking, and on-chain monitoring tools help track transaction performance, network stability, and potential security threats. In the event of unexpected issues, emergency response mechanisms, such as contract upgradeability (if supported) or governance-driven fixes, should be in place.

A smooth deployment also requires strategic user onboarding and liquidity management. Token projects should ensure that sufficient liquidity is provided on decentralized exchanges (DEXs) or centralized exchanges (CEXs) for trading. Proper documentation, user guides, and community support enhance adoption and trust in the cryptocurrency.

Testing and deployment require meticulous attention to detail, balancing security, efficiency, and usability. By following best practices, developers can launch a robust, secure, and scalable cryptocurrency that stands the test of time. Continuous monitoring and iterative improvements ensure that the project remains competitive and resilient in an evolving blockchain landscape.

Chapter 5
Setting Up a Blockchain Network

Setting up a blockchain network is a critical step in launching a cryptocurrency, requiring careful planning, infrastructure deployment, and security measures. Whether developing a private, public, or consortium blockchain, the setup process involves configuring nodes, implementing a consensus mechanism, and ensuring network stability. A well-structured blockchain network provides security, scalability, and efficiency, allowing seamless transactions and decentralized governance.

The first step in setting up a blockchain network is choosing the network type. Public blockchains, like Bitcoin and Ethereum, are decentralized and open to anyone, while private blockchains restrict access to specific participants. Consortium blockchains, such as those used by enterprises, allow multiple organizations to govern the network collectively. The choice of network type impacts scalability, security, and regulatory compliance.

Next, developers must configure nodes, the computers that maintain the blockchain ledger. Nodes validate transactions, store blockchain history, and secure the network against attacks. Setting up a full node involves installing the blockchain software, syncing with the network, and ensuring a reliable internet connection. Validator nodes, required for Proof of Stake (PoS) and Delegated Proof of Stake

(DPoS) networks, must meet specific staking requirements to participate in consensus.

The consensus mechanism determines how transactions are validated and blocks are added to the chain. Options include Proof of Work (PoW), Proof of Stake (PoS), and hybrid models. PoW, used by Bitcoin, requires high computational power, making it secure but energy-intensive. PoS and Delegated PoS (DPoS) provide faster and more efficient alternatives, reducing energy consumption while maintaining decentralization.

Security measures are essential when setting up a blockchain network. Implementing encryption protocols, private key management, and access control prevents unauthorized modifications and protects user data. Networks should have protection against 51% attacks, Sybil attacks, and DDoS threats. Blockchain firewalls, multi-signature authentication, and regular security audits enhance network integrity.

After configuring security, the next step is setting up genesis blocks, which define the initial state of the blockchain. The genesis block contains network parameters, such as token distribution, initial validators, and governance rules. Developers must ensure that the genesis block is correctly formatted, as any errors require restarting the network from scratch.

Scalability solutions should be integrated from the beginning. Layer-2 solutions, such as sharding, rollups, and sidechains, improve transaction throughput and reduce congestion. Networks planning to support high-frequency transactions, such as DeFi applications or gaming platforms, should optimize block size, confirmation times, and gas fee structures.

Once the blockchain is operational, testing and monitoring become critical. Developers should deploy test transactions, validate block production, and monitor network health. Tools like blockchain explorers, real-time analytics dashboards, and logging systems help track performance and detect anomalies. Continuous updates and security patches ensure that the network remains resilient to evolving threats.

For blockchain networks intended for public use, community engagement and governance mechanisms play a crucial role. Decentralized governance models, such as Decentralized Autonomous Organizations (DAOs), enable community-driven decision-making. Proper documentation, developer tools, and support channels encourage participation and long-term sustainability.

Setting up a blockchain network requires a comprehensive approach, balancing security, efficiency, scalability, and governance. A well-structured network provides the foundation for a successful cryptocurrency, enabling trustless transactions and decentralized applications. By following best practices, blockchain developers can create a robust and scalable ecosystem that meets the needs of users and businesses alike.

Nodes and Validators: How They Work

Nodes and validators are essential components of a blockchain network, responsible for maintaining security, validating transactions, and ensuring network integrity. They form the backbone of decentralized systems, preventing fraud, enabling consensus, and keeping the blockchain operational. Understanding how nodes and validators work helps in designing a robust and secure blockchain infrastructure.

A node is any computer connected to the blockchain network that stores a copy of the distributed ledger and participates in transaction verification. Nodes ensure that all transactions comply with network rules, preventing double-spending and unauthorized modifications. There are different types of nodes, each serving a unique function in the network.

Full nodes store the entire blockchain history and validate new transactions and blocks. They ensure the integrity of the blockchain by verifying digital signatures and enforcing protocol rules. Running a full node requires significant storage and processing power, as it must download and process all past and future transactions.

Light nodes do not store the full blockchain history but instead rely on full nodes for transaction verification. They are designed for users who need quick access to blockchain data without the burden of maintaining large storage. Light nodes are commonly used in mobile wallets and applications that require blockchain interaction without running a full client.

Masternodes provide additional functionalities, such as instant transactions, private transactions, and governance features. Unlike full nodes, masternodes do not add new blocks to the blockchain but play a crucial role in network stability and decision-making. To run a masternode, participants must hold a certain amount of cryptocurrency as collateral, ensuring that they have a vested interest in the network's security.

A validator is a special type of node responsible for confirming transactions and adding new blocks to the blockchain. Validators are used in Proof of Stake (PoS) and Delegated Proof of Stake (DPoS) networks instead of traditional miners. In PoS systems, validators are selected based on the number of tokens they hold and are willing to "stake" as collateral. The more tokens staked, the higher the chance of being chosen to validate transactions and earn rewards.

In Delegated Proof of Stake (DPoS), token holders vote for a limited number of validators to secure the network on their behalf. These elected validators are responsible for block production and network governance. DPoS improves transaction speed and scalability but introduces an element of centralization since only a small group of validators controls block production.

Validators play a crucial role in network security by ensuring that only valid transactions are included in the blockchain. They follow consensus rules, prevent fraudulent transactions, and maintain blockchain consistency. If a validator acts maliciously or fails to follow network rules, they may lose their staked tokens as a penalty, a process known as slashing.

The decentralization of nodes and validators impacts the security and resilience of a blockchain. A widely distributed network of nodes prevents single points of failure, ensuring that no single entity controls the blockchain. More validators lead to greater security, making it harder for bad actors to manipulate the ledger.

Running a node or validator requires technical expertise, hardware resources, and, in some cases, financial commitment. Full nodes require high storage capacity, while validators must stake cryptocurrency to participate in block validation. Proper node synchronization, uptime maintenance, and security measures are necessary to ensure network stability.

Nodes and validators are fundamental to blockchain operations, enabling decentralized verification and consensus. While nodes maintain the integrity of the ledger, validators actively secure and validate new transactions. The choice between running a full node, a validator, or a masternode depends on the level of participation required and the blockchain's consensus mechanism. A well-distributed network of nodes and validators strengthens blockchain security, ensuring trust, transparency, and decentralization.

Configuring a Peer-to-Peer Network

Configuring a peer-to-peer (P2P) network is an essential step in establishing a decentralized blockchain system. P2P networks eliminate the need for a central authority by enabling direct communication between nodes, ensuring data distribution, security, and consensus. A well-configured P2P network enhances blockchain efficiency, transaction validation, and fault tolerance, making it the backbone of any decentralized ecosystem.

The first step in setting up a P2P network is defining the network topology. Blockchain networks typically follow a decentralized, distributed architecture where each node communicates with multiple peers. Unlike traditional client-server models, where data is stored in centralized locations, P2P networks allow all participating nodes to share and verify transactions independently. This prevents single points of failure and enhances system resilience.

Node discovery mechanisms determine how new nodes connect to the network. When a node joins a blockchain, it must find existing nodes to establish connections. Some blockchains use hardcoded seed nodes, which are predefined entry points that help new nodes find peers. Others use peer discovery protocols, where nodes share information about active peers dynamically, ensuring network connectivity even if some nodes go offline.

Once a node connects to the network, it starts synchronizing the blockchain ledger. Full nodes download and verify the entire blockchain history, while light nodes request relevant transaction data from full nodes. Synchronization ensures that all nodes maintain an updated, tamper-proof ledger. Efficient data propagation is achieved through gossip protocols, where nodes relay information to connected peers until the entire network is updated.

Network security measures play a crucial role in preventing attacks on the P2P infrastructure. Blockchain networks must protect against Sybil attacks, where malicious actors create multiple fake nodes to manipulate consensus, and eclipse attacks, where an attacker isolates a node by controlling all its peer connections. Implementing peer reputation systems, banning misbehaving nodes, and using cryptographic authentication enhances network integrity.

Blockchain P2P networks rely on message propagation protocols to ensure efficient data distribution. Transactions and blocks must be broadcasted to the network in a timely manner to maintain consensus. Some blockchains use flooding techniques, where each node relays messages to all its peers, while others optimize bandwidth by selectively forwarding transactions based on network load and priority.

To improve scalability and efficiency, some blockchain networks implement overlay networks or Layer-2 solutions. These solutions reduce congestion on the main blockchain by handling smaller transactions off-chain while maintaining a secure connection to the main ledger. Technologies like state channels, sidechains, and sharding enhance transaction throughput without compromising security.

Configuring network parameters, such as block size, transaction limits, and connection thresholds, ensures optimal performance. Blockchain networks must balance security, decentralization, and speed when setting these parameters. A well-configured P2P network prevents network congestion, reduces latency, and ensures smooth transaction processing.

Monitoring and maintaining a P2P blockchain network require real-time analytics and logging tools. Node operators use diagnostic software to track peer connections, data synchronization rates, and potential security threats. Regular software updates and optimizations help maintain network stability and performance.

A properly configured P2P network ensures a decentralized, secure, and efficient blockchain ecosystem. By establishing effective peer discovery, secure communication channels, optimized data propagation, and scalability solutions, developers can create a robust infrastructure for blockchain applications. As blockchain adoption grows, advancements in P2P networking will continue to enhance the performance and security of decentralized systems.

Security and Encryption Protocols

Security and encryption protocols are fundamental to blockchain networks, ensuring transaction integrity, data confidentiality, and protection against malicious attacks. A well-secured blockchain ecosystem relies on cryptographic techniques, consensus mechanisms, and network security protocols to maintain decentralization while preventing unauthorized access and tampering. Implementing strong security measures is crucial for sustaining trust in cryptocurrency and decentralized applications.

The foundation of blockchain security lies in cryptographic encryption. Public-key cryptography, also known as asymmetric encryption, is used to secure transactions. Each user has a public key, which is openly shared, and a private key, which is kept secret. When a transaction is initiated, the sender signs it using their private key, and nodes in the network verify the authenticity using the sender's public key. This ensures that only the rightful owner can authorize transactions, preventing forgery and fraud. The Elliptic Curve Digital Signature Algorithm (ECDSA) is commonly used in blockchain networks like Bitcoin and Ethereum for digital signatures, ensuring strong security while maintaining efficiency.

Hashing algorithms play a crucial role in maintaining blockchain integrity. Each block in a blockchain contains a cryptographic hash of the previous block, creating a chain that prevents data manipulation. Hash functions, such as SHA-256 (Bitcoin) and Keccak-256 (Ethereum), generate unique, fixed-length hashes for transaction data. Any modification to transaction records alters the hash, making tampering easily detectable. Hashing also secures user passwords, ensures block immutability, and optimizes data verification processes.

Consensus mechanisms further enhance blockchain security by preventing double-spending and unauthorized modifications. Proof of Work (PoW), used by Bitcoin, requires miners to solve complex mathematical puzzles to validate transactions. This computationally intensive process makes it nearly impossible for attackers to alter previous blocks. Proof of Stake (PoS) and its variations, such as Delegated Proof of Stake (DPoS) and Practical Byzantine Fault Tolerance (PBFT), secure networks by selecting validators based on their stake in the network, reducing energy consumption while maintaining security.

To protect blockchain networks from Sybil attacks, where malicious actors create multiple fake identities to gain control, blockchain protocols use identity verification mechanisms like staking requirements or peer reputation systems. Eclipse attacks, where an attacker isolates a node by controlling all its peer connections, are mitigated by implementing diverse peer selection strategies and limiting direct connections to a single entity.

End-to-end encryption ensures secure communication between nodes. Transport Layer Security (TLS) and Secure Sockets Layer (SSL) encrypt data during transmission, preventing eavesdropping and man-in-the-middle attacks. Blockchain networks also use Virtual Private Networks (VPNs) and Tor-based routing for additional privacy and protection.

Smart contract security is another critical area, as vulnerabilities in smart contract code can lead to hacks and financial losses. Common smart contract attacks include reentrancy exploits, integer overflows, front-running, and unauthorized access. Implementing secure coding practices, using well-audited libraries, and performing formal verification reduces the risk of vulnerabilities. Projects often undergo third-party security audits by firms such as CertiK, OpenZeppelin, and Trail of Bits to ensure smart contract integrity.

To enhance user security, blockchain networks implement multi-signature (multi-sig) wallets, requiring multiple approvals before executing transactions. Hierarchical Deterministic (HD) wallets provide additional protection by generating unique addresses for each transaction, reducing the risk of address reuse and tracking.

Quantum computing poses a future threat to blockchain encryption, as quantum computers could potentially break existing cryptographic algorithms. Some blockchain projects are exploring quantum-resistant encryption techniques, such as lattice-based cryptography, to future-proof blockchain security.

Regular network monitoring and threat detection play a vital role in maintaining security. Blockchain analytics tools track suspicious activity, detect unusual transaction patterns, and prevent fraudulent behavior. Decentralized security models, such as bug bounty programs and community-driven governance, help identify vulnerabilities before they can be exploited.

Security and encryption protocols are essential for protecting blockchain networks from fraud, hacks, and cyber threats. By leveraging advanced cryptographic methods, consensus algorithms, smart contract best practices, and real-time monitoring, blockchain projects can ensure a secure, decentralized, and trustless environment. As cyber threats evolve, continuous security enhancements and innovations will be key to maintaining blockchain integrity and reliability.

Ensuring Decentralization and Scalability

Ensuring decentralization and scalability in a blockchain network is essential for maintaining security, efficiency, and widespread adoption. A well-balanced blockchain must achieve decentralization to prevent central control while also scaling effectively to handle increasing transaction volumes without compromising speed or cost. Striking this balance is one of the biggest challenges in blockchain development, as decentralization can often slow down transaction processing, while excessive centralization can make the network vulnerable to attacks and manipulation.

Decentralization ensures that no single entity or group controls the network, preventing censorship and enhancing security. In a decentralized blockchain, transactions are verified by a distributed network of nodes, reducing the risk of fraud or corruption. To achieve decentralization, blockchains use various consensus mechanisms, such as Proof of Work (PoW), Proof of Stake (PoS), Delegated Proof of Stake (DPoS), and Byzantine Fault Tolerance (BFT) algorithms. PoW, used by Bitcoin, is highly decentralized because mining power is distributed among multiple participants. However, it is energy-intensive and can limit scalability. PoS and DPoS improve efficiency by allowing validators to secure the network based on the number of tokens staked, but these models can introduce some level of centralization if a small group controls a large share of the stake.

To further decentralize a blockchain, it is essential to have a widely distributed network of nodes and validators. The more geographically and operationally diverse the nodes are, the harder it becomes for any single entity to manipulate the network. Decentralized governance models, such as Decentralized Autonomous Organizations (DAOs), enable community-driven decision-making, ensuring that protocol upgrades and rule changes are not controlled by a small group of developers or stakeholders.

Scalability refers to a blockchain's ability to handle high transaction volumes while maintaining low fees and fast processing times. Many early blockchains, such as Bitcoin and Ethereum, struggle with scalability due to network congestion and limited transaction throughput. As transaction volumes increase, fees rise, and processing speeds slow down, creating barriers to mass adoption.

Several scalability solutions have been developed to address these issues. Layer-2 solutions, such as Lightning Network for Bitcoin and Rollups (Optimistic and Zero-Knowledge) for Ethereum, enable transactions to be processed off-chain while settling final transaction data on the main blockchain. These solutions significantly reduce congestion and transaction costs while maintaining security.

Sharding is another approach to scalability, dividing the blockchain into smaller partitions, or "shards," that process transactions independently. Ethereum 2.0 is adopting sharding to improve transaction speeds and reduce network congestion.

Sidechains and interoperability protocols, such as Polkadot's parachains and Cosmos' Inter-Blockchain Communication (IBC) protocol, enable separate blockchains to communicate and share transaction loads, enhancing overall scalability.

The block size debate is another aspect of scalability. Larger block sizes allow more transactions per block, increasing throughput, but they also require more storage and processing power, which can lead to centralization. Bitcoin Cash increased its block size to improve transaction capacity, while Bitcoin maintained smaller blocks to prioritize decentralization.

Optimizing network latency and consensus efficiency is crucial for scaling blockchain networks. Some projects, like Solana, use a Proof of History (PoH) consensus mechanism, which timestamps transactions before validation, allowing higher speeds while maintaining security. Other blockchains, such as Algorand, use Pure Proof of Stake (PPoS) to achieve near-instant finality with minimal computational overhead.

Decentralization and scalability must be carefully balanced to maintain security, efficiency, and accessibility. While decentralization ensures a trustless and censorship-resistant network, scalability is necessary for widespread adoption and usability. By integrating Layer-2 solutions, sharding, sidechains, and optimized consensus mechanisms, blockchain projects can build networks that are both highly decentralized and capable of handling large-scale transactions efficiently. Continuous innovation in blockchain architecture will drive the next generation of scalable, decentralized ecosystems that can support global financial systems, enterprise applications, and Web3 services.

Chapter 6
Creating a Crypto Wallet

Creating a crypto wallet is a fundamental step in cryptocurrency development, enabling users to securely store, send, and receive digital assets. A well-designed crypto wallet must prioritize security, usability, compatibility, and accessibility to ensure a seamless user experience while safeguarding private keys and transactions. The wallet type, architecture, and cryptographic security mechanisms must be carefully selected to align with the intended blockchain ecosystem.

The first step in developing a crypto wallet is choosing the wallet type. Crypto wallets fall into two main categories: hot wallets and cold wallets. Hot wallets are connected to the internet and are suitable for frequent transactions, while cold wallets are offline, providing enhanced security against cyber threats. Hot wallets include mobile, desktop, and web wallets, while cold wallets include hardware and paper wallets.

Wallets can also be categorized based on custodianship. Non-custodial wallets give users full control over their private keys, enhancing security and decentralization. Examples include MetaMask, Trust Wallet, and hardware wallets like Ledger and Trezor. Custodial wallets, on the other hand, are managed by third-party services, such as cryptocurrency exchanges, where users rely on the provider for security and private key management.

Developing a wallet requires implementing public-key cryptography to enable secure transactions. Each wallet generates a public key (wallet address) and a private key, which acts as a digital signature for authorizing transactions. Elliptic Curve Digital Signature Algorithm (ECDSA) and Ed25519 cryptographic standards are commonly used to generate these keys securely.

To enhance security, wallets should incorporate seed phrase recovery mechanisms. A 12-word or 24-word mnemonic phrase, following the BIP-39 standard, allows users to restore their wallet in case of device loss. Proper key derivation using BIP-32 hierarchical deterministic (HD) wallets ensures that multiple addresses can be generated from a single seed phrase while maintaining security.

The next step is wallet integration with a blockchain network. The wallet must be able to interact with blockchain nodes to broadcast transactions and verify balances. Light wallets, also known as SPV (Simplified Payment Verification) wallets, do not download the entire blockchain but instead query full nodes to verify transactions, improving efficiency. Full-node wallets, like Bitcoin Core, store the entire blockchain, providing enhanced security but requiring more storage.

Smart contract integration is essential for wallets that support Ethereum-based tokens (ERC-20, ERC-721, ERC-1155) or other blockchain standards. APIs like Web3.js, Ethers.js, and Binance's BSC SDK allow wallets to interact with decentralized applications (dApps), execute smart contracts, and manage multi-asset transactions.

Security is a top priority in crypto wallet development. Wallets must use end-to-end encryption, multi-signature (multi-sig) authentication, and biometric security to prevent unauthorized access. Implementing hardware security module (HSM) support further enhances private key protection. Wallets should also incorporate anti-phishing protection, such as domain verification and transaction confirmation pop-ups, to prevent scams.

For usability, wallets must offer an intuitive interface, transaction history tracking, and real-time balance updates. Features like QR code scanning, push notifications, and fiat conversion rates improve the user experience. Multi-chain support allows wallets to manage assets from multiple blockchain networks, increasing versatility.

After development, wallets must undergo extensive security audits and penetration testing to identify vulnerabilities before public release. Open-source wallets encourage transparency and community-driven security enhancements.

Deploying a crypto wallet involves publishing it on relevant platforms, such as mobile app stores for iOS and Android wallets, or making desktop versions available for Windows, macOS, and Linux users. Web wallets should use secure HTTPS connections and Content Security Policy (CSP) measures to prevent attacks.

A well-structured crypto wallet balances security, decentralization, usability, and interoperability. By implementing strong cryptographic protections, seamless blockchain integration, and user-friendly interfaces, developers can create a secure and efficient wallet for managing digital assets. As the cryptocurrency space evolves, wallet security and functionality must continuously adapt to emerging threats and user needs, ensuring long-term trust and reliability.

Types of Wallets: Hot, Cold, and Hardware Wallets

Crypto wallets are essential for storing, sending, and receiving cryptocurrencies securely. They come in different types based on their connectivity and security levels: hot wallets, cold wallets, and hardware wallets. Each type has its own advantages and trade-offs in terms of convenience, security, and usability.

Hot wallets are connected to the internet, making them easily accessible but more vulnerable to cyber threats. These wallets are ideal for frequent transactions, trading, and interacting with decentralized applications (dApps). Hot wallets include web wallets, mobile wallets, and desktop wallets. Web wallets are browser-based and hosted by third-party providers, offering convenience but requiring users to trust the service provider's security. Mobile wallets, like Trust Wallet and MetaMask, provide portability and quick access, often integrating with dApps and decentralized exchanges. Desktop wallets, such as Electrum and Exodus, run on personal computers, giving users more control but requiring regular security updates to prevent malware attacks. Since hot wallets are online, they are susceptible to phishing attacks, keylogging, and hacking attempts.

Cold wallets operate offline, offering enhanced security by keeping private keys away from potential online threats. These wallets are ideal for long-term storage and protecting large cryptocurrency holdings. Paper wallets are a type of cold wallet where private and public keys are printed on a physical piece of paper. While highly secure against hacking, paper wallets can be lost, damaged, or stolen if not stored properly. Air-gapped computers, which never connect to the internet, can also function as cold wallets by generating and signing transactions offline before broadcasting them through another device.

Hardware wallets are a specialized type of cold wallet that combines offline security with convenience. These physical devices, such as Ledger, Trezor, and KeepKey, store private keys securely and require physical confirmation to authorize transactions. Hardware wallets protect against malware and hacking attempts, as private keys never leave the device. They use secure elements and PIN protection to safeguard funds. Although highly secure, hardware wallets must be purchased, and users must ensure proper backup procedures in case of device loss or failure.

Choosing the right wallet depends on security needs, convenience, and usage frequency. Hot wallets are best for daily transactions and DeFi interactions but require strict security measures. Cold wallets provide superior security for long-term holdings but lack instant accessibility. Hardware wallets offer a balanced solution, combining security with usability. Using a combination of hot and cold wallets allows users to optimize security while maintaining easy access to funds. As cryptocurrency adoption grows, wallet security remains a top priority, ensuring that users can safely manage their digital assets.

Generating Private and Public Keys

Generating private and public keys is a fundamental process in blockchain and cryptocurrency security. These cryptographic keys enable secure transactions, digital signatures, and ownership verification of assets on a blockchain network. The process of key generation relies on asymmetric cryptography, ensuring that private keys remain confidential while public keys are shared openly.

A private key is a randomly generated number that acts as the ultimate proof of ownership for a cryptocurrency wallet. It is used to sign transactions, proving that the sender has the authority to transfer funds. Private keys are typically 256-bit numbers, making them nearly impossible to guess or brute-force attack. In Bitcoin and Ethereum, private keys are generated using secp256k1 elliptic curve cryptography (ECC), which ensures security and efficiency.

A public key is derived from the private key through an irreversible cryptographic function. This public key is then used to generate a wallet address, which serves as an identifier for receiving funds. The relationship between the private key and the public key is one-way, meaning that while a public key can be derived from a private key, the reverse operation is computationally infeasible.

The process of generating a key pair follows these steps:

1. Generating the Private Key – A large random number (256-bit for Bitcoin and Ethereum) is created using a cryptographically secure random number generator (CSPRNG).

2. Deriving the Public Key – The private key is used in an elliptic curve multiplication process to generate the corresponding public key.

3. Creating the Wallet Address – The public key undergoes hashing and encoding (SHA-256 and RIPEMD-160 in Bitcoin) to generate a shorter, user-friendly wallet address.

To enhance security, private keys can be stored using mnemonic seed phrases, following the BIP-39 standard. This allows users to recover their wallets using a 12-word or 24-word phrase, reducing the risk of key loss. Hierarchical Deterministic (HD) wallets use BIP-32 and BIP-44 standards to generate multiple addresses from a single seed, improving privacy and usability.

Proper private key management is crucial. Losing a private key means losing access to funds, as no central authority can restore it. Private keys should be stored securely using hardware wallets, encrypted backups, or offline cold storage. Never share or expose private keys, as anyone who gains access can control the associated funds.

Public and private key cryptography underpins the security of blockchain transactions, ensuring that ownership and authentication remain trustless and decentralized. By following best practices for key generation and storage, users can protect their digital assets while securely interacting with blockchain networks.

Security Best Practices for Wallet Development

Developing a secure crypto wallet requires implementing best practices that protect users' private keys, transactions, and funds from cyber threats. Poor security measures can result in hacks, unauthorized access, or permanent loss of assets. A well-designed wallet should prioritize encryption, authentication, secure key storage, and user protection to ensure maximum security.

The most critical security aspect of wallet development is private key management. Private keys should never be stored in plaintext or transmitted over the internet. Instead, wallets should use hardware security modules (HSMs), secure enclaves, or key vaults to protect sensitive cryptographic data. Hierarchical Deterministic (HD) wallets, following BIP-32 and BIP-44 standards, allow for the secure generation of multiple keys from a single master seed, improving both security and usability.

Using end-to-end encryption (E2EE) is essential for securing wallet data. AES-256 encryption ensures that private keys, seed phrases, and wallet credentials remain protected, even if attackers gain access to a device. Encrypting wallet backups and storing them offline prevents unauthorized access in case of data breaches.

Strong authentication mechanisms enhance security. Implementing multi-factor authentication (MFA) using time-based one-time passwords (TOTP) or biometric authentication adds an extra layer of protection. Wallets should also enforce strong password policies, requiring users to create complex and unique passwords.

For online wallets, secure communication protocols must be used to prevent data interception. TLS/SSL encryption should be applied to all wallet-related communications. Domain verification mechanisms and anti-phishing protections help users identify legitimate wallet applications and prevent social engineering attacks.

To prevent unauthorized transactions, wallets should implement multi-signature (multi-sig) security. Multi-sig wallets require multiple approvals before executing transactions, reducing the risk of a single compromised key leading to fund theft. Time-locked transactions and spending limits provide additional safeguards.

A secure wallet must also include transaction verification and anti-replay protection. Users should be able to review transaction details before signing, ensuring that funds are sent to the intended recipient. Implementing nonce management prevents transaction replays and double-spending attacks.

Open-source development and third-party security audits help ensure wallet security. Reputable blockchain security firms like CertiK, OpenZeppelin, and Trail of Bits conduct comprehensive audits to identify vulnerabilities before deployment. Open-source wallets allow the developer community to inspect and improve security protocols.

Regular software updates and security patches are crucial for maintaining wallet security. Wallet providers must actively monitor emerging threats and update codebases to address vulnerabilities. Implementing auto-update mechanisms with cryptographic signature verification prevents tampering.

For maximum security, users should be encouraged to store backups of their seed phrases offline using cold storage solutions, such as paper backups or hardware wallets. Secure recovery mechanisms should ensure that users can restore access to their wallets without exposing private keys to potential attackers.

By following best practices such as private key encryption, multi-factor authentication, secure communication protocols, smart contract audits, and continuous monitoring, crypto wallet developers can create secure, user-friendly solutions. Proper security implementations protect users from phishing attacks, malware, and unauthorized access, ensuring a reliable and trustworthy cryptocurrency storage solution.

Integrating Wallets with Your Cryptocurrency

Integrating wallets with a cryptocurrency is a crucial step in ensuring seamless transactions, secure asset management, and user accessibility. A properly integrated wallet allows users to store, send, and receive tokens while interacting with decentralized applications (dApps), exchanges, and blockchain services. The integration process involves ensuring compatibility with blockchain protocols, security implementation, and user-friendly interfaces to enhance adoption and usability.

The first step in wallet integration is choosing the wallet type that aligns with the cryptocurrency's purpose. Hot wallets (web, mobile, and desktop) offer easy access and frequent transactions, while cold wallets (hardware and offline storage) provide maximum security for long-term holdings. Multi-chain wallets support multiple blockchain networks, increasing interoperability and accessibility.

To enable wallet functionality, developers must connect the wallet to the blockchain network using APIs and SDKs. Wallets interact with blockchain nodes to broadcast transactions, verify balances, and retrieve blockchain data. Projects can use JSON-RPC, Web3.js (for Ethereum-based tokens), or Bitcoin's RPC API for blockchain communication. Decentralized applications typically use Ethers.js, Binance Chain SDK, or Solana Web3.js to facilitate wallet transactions.

Cryptocurrency wallets must support the native coin and any token standards used on the blockchain. For Ethereum and Binance Smart Chain, wallets must be ERC-20, ERC-721 (NFTs), and BEP-20 compliant to interact with smart contracts. Similarly, integrating support for Solana SPL tokens, TRC-20 (Tron), or custom blockchain assets ensures broader usability.

Security is a top priority when integrating wallets. Private keys must never be exposed or stored on centralized servers. Instead, wallets should use mnemonic phrases (BIP-39), hardware security modules (HSMs), and secure key vaults for encryption. End-to-end encryption, biometric authentication, and multi-signature transactions add additional layers of protection.

For seamless user experience, wallets should implement QR code scanning, push notifications, and fiat conversion rates. Features like gas fee estimation, transaction previews, and one-click token swaps enhance usability. Wallets should also support multi-account management and custom RPC endpoints for advanced users.

Integration with hardware wallets like Ledger and Trezor adds an extra layer of security. Hardware wallets interact with software wallets via U2F (Universal 2nd Factor) authentication and USB/Bluetooth interfaces, allowing users to sign transactions without exposing private keys.

To support decentralized finance (DeFi) applications, wallets should be compatible with smart contract interactions. Connecting with Metamask, Trust Wallet, Coinbase Wallet, and WalletConnect enables users to participate in DeFi lending, staking, and yield farming. Open-source wallet libraries, such as WalletConnect and Web3Modal, allow seamless dApp connectivity across multiple wallets.

Ensuring cross-platform compatibility enables wider adoption. Mobile wallets should be optimized for iOS (Swift) and Android (Kotlin, Java), while web wallets should be compatible with major browsers. Wallet extensions, like Metamask, provide a bridge between users and dApps, making transactions more accessible.

Testing and security audits are critical before deploying a wallet integration. Developers should conduct smart contract security audits, penetration testing, and load testing to identify vulnerabilities. Wallet transactions must be validated on testnets (e.g., Ethereum Goerli, Binance Testnet) before going live on the main network.

By implementing secure blockchain interactions, multi-wallet support, and strong cryptographic protections, cryptocurrency projects can ensure smooth wallet integration. A well-integrated wallet enhances the overall user experience, strengthens security, and increases adoption, positioning the cryptocurrency for broader market success.

Chapter 7
Launching an Initial Coin Offering (ICO) or Token Sale

Launching an Initial Coin Offering (ICO) or token sale is a strategic process that enables blockchain projects to raise capital by distributing tokens to investors and users. A successful ICO requires careful planning, legal compliance, a well-designed tokenomics model, and a strong marketing strategy to attract participants. Since ICOs have been scrutinized due to regulatory concerns and fraudulent schemes, ensuring transparency and security is essential for long-term credibility and investor confidence.

The first step in launching an ICO is defining the purpose and utility of the token. Tokens should have a clear role within the ecosystem, whether as a utility token (used for platform services), a governance token (providing voting rights), or a security token (representing ownership in a company or asset). The token should follow a widely accepted standard, such as ERC-20 (Ethereum), BEP-20 (Binance Smart Chain), or Solana SPL tokens, to ensure compatibility with wallets and exchanges.

Creating a comprehensive whitepaper is crucial for communicating the project's vision, technical architecture, use cases, tokenomics, and roadmap. A well-structured whitepaper should explain how the project solves a real-world problem, the technology behind it, and the benefits for investors and users. The document should also outline the ICO structure, including the number of tokens to be sold, pricing strategy, and fundraising goals.

Legal and regulatory compliance is a critical aspect of launching an ICO. Since ICOs operate in a global environment, projects must adhere to the regulations of the jurisdictions they target. Some countries have strict rules on cryptocurrency fundraising, classifying ICOs as securities offerings subject to financial regulations. Conducting a legal assessment and consulting with blockchain attorneys help ensure compliance with laws such as KYC (Know Your Customer), AML (Anti-Money Laundering), and securities regulations. Establishing a clear terms and conditions agreement protects the project and its investors.

The next step is developing the ICO smart contract to handle token issuance and distribution securely. The smart contract should enforce hard caps, soft caps, vesting schedules, refund mechanisms, and token allocations. Security best practices, including multi-signature wallets, contract audits, and real-time monitoring, help prevent vulnerabilities. Reputable audit firms like CertiK, OpenZeppelin, and Trail of Bits should conduct security audits before deployment.

Setting up a fundraising platform and payment methods ensures smooth participation in the ICO. Investors should be able to purchase tokens using cryptocurrencies (BTC, ETH, BNB, USDT) and fiat. Using escrow mechanisms or smart contract-based fund management enhances transparency and investor trust.

A marketing and community engagement strategy is essential to attract investors and build credibility. A strong presence on social media (Twitter, Telegram, Discord, LinkedIn, Medium), cryptocurrency forums (BitcoinTalk, Reddit), and ICO listing platforms increases visibility. Conducting airdrop campaigns, influencer partnerships, and press releases helps generate buzz. Transparency, active community engagement, and regular updates keep investors informed and motivated.

The ICO launch is typically divided into phases, including private sales, pre-sale, and public sale. Private sales allow early investors to buy tokens at discounted rates, while pre-sales offer tokens at a lower price before the public sale. Some projects implement vesting schedules to prevent early investors from dumping tokens and affecting market stability.

After the ICO, ensuring liquidity and exchange listings is crucial for token adoption. Listing the token on decentralized exchanges (DEXs) like Uniswap, PancakeSwap, and SushiSwap, as well as centralized exchanges (CEXs) like Binance, Coinbase, and Kraken, provides accessibility. Partnerships with market makers improve liquidity, while integrating the token into DeFi platforms, staking, and governance mechanisms enhances long-term utility.

A well-planned ICO balances legal compliance, security, tokenomics, investor engagement, and liquidity strategies to ensure a successful fundraising campaign. By following best practices, blockchain projects can attract investment, build a strong community, and sustain long-term growth in the competitive cryptocurrency space.

ICO vs. IDO vs. IEO: Understanding the Differences

When launching a cryptocurrency project, choosing the right fundraising method is crucial for attracting investors and ensuring a successful token launch. The three most common token sale models are Initial Coin Offering (ICO), Initial Exchange Offering (IEO), and Initial DEX Offering (IDO). Each method has distinct features, benefits, and risks, making it essential to understand their differences before selecting the best approach.

Initial Coin Offering (ICO) was the first widely used method for blockchain fundraising, allowing projects to raise capital by selling tokens directly to investors. ICOs are decentralized and not managed by exchanges, meaning the project team handles the entire process, from token creation and marketing to sales and distribution. Investors typically purchase tokens using cryptocurrencies like Bitcoin (BTC) or Ethereum (ETH). ICOs gained massive popularity in 2017-2018 but later faced scrutiny due to fraudulent projects and lack of regulation.

ICO Advantages:

- Full control over the fundraising process without relying on third parties.
- Global participation with minimal restrictions.
- Lower costs compared to exchange-managed token sales.

ICO Disadvantages:

- Regulatory uncertainty in many jurisdictions, leading to potential legal issues.
- Higher risks for investors due to scams and lack of transparency.
- Marketing and trust-building challenges, as the project must prove its legitimacy independently.

Initial Exchange Offering (IEO) is a more secure fundraising method where the token sale is conducted through a centralized cryptocurrency exchange (CEX). The exchange acts as a middleman, conducting due diligence on the project before listing it on its platform. Investors participate in the token sale directly through the exchange, increasing trust and reducing the risk of scams.

IEO Advantages:

- Increased credibility since exchanges vet the projects before launching.
- Built-in investor base from the exchange's user community.
- Exchange listing is guaranteed, providing liquidity immediately after the sale.

IEO Disadvantages:

- High listing fees as exchanges charge significant amounts to host an IEO.
- Centralized control, reducing the project's independence.
- Regulatory risks, as exchanges must comply with government regulations.

Initial DEX Offering (IDO) is a fundraising method conducted on decentralized exchanges (DEXs) instead of centralized platforms. In an IDO, tokens are launched via liquidity pools on automated market makers (AMMs) like Uniswap (Ethereum), PancakeSwap (Binance Smart Chain), and Raydium (Solana). Unlike ICOs and IEOs, IDOs provide immediate token liquidity, enabling investors to trade tokens as soon as they are launched.

IDO Advantages:

- Decentralized and permissionless, reducing regulatory risks.

- Instant liquidity as tokens are listed on DEXs immediately.
- Lower costs since no large fees are paid to centralized exchanges.

IDO Disadvantages:

- Less investor protection, as DEXs do not conduct extensive due diligence.
- Price volatility, as tokens can experience sharp price swings due to liquidity constraints.
- Potential for bots and front-running attacks, where automated traders buy tokens before retail investors and sell at higher prices.

Choosing the Right Fundraising Method

- ICO is suitable for projects that want full control over fundraising but must build credibility and handle regulatory concerns.
- IEO is ideal for projects seeking credibility and exposure through an exchange but willing to pay high listing fees.
- IDO is best for projects that prioritize decentralization and liquidity but are prepared to handle volatility and security risks.

As blockchain fundraising evolves, new models like Initial Game Offering (IGO) and Security Token Offering (STO) are emerging, offering different benefits and regulatory frameworks. Understanding the strengths and weaknesses of ICOs, IEOs, and IDOs allows projects to select the most effective method for their token launch strategy.

Creating a Whitepaper and Roadmap

Creating a whitepaper and roadmap is an essential step in launching a successful cryptocurrency project. The whitepaper serves as a detailed document outlining the project's vision, problem statement, technical architecture, tokenomics, governance model, and future development plans. It acts as a guide for investors, developers, and users, providing transparency and credibility. A well-structured whitepaper explains how the blockchain technology is utilized, the real-world problem it aims to solve, and how its token functions within the ecosystem. It should also include an analysis of the target market, competitors, and adoption potential to demonstrate the project's long-term viability.

A strong whitepaper clearly defines the tokenomics model, specifying the total supply, token distribution strategy, staking or reward mechanisms, and fund allocation. This section ensures that investors understand the financial model of the project, including how tokens are issued, how they gain value, and what incentives exist for holding or using them. Compliance and legal considerations should also be addressed to reassure investors that the project follows relevant regulatory frameworks such as KYC, AML, and securities laws. Smart contract audit plans, security measures, and governance structures, including decentralized decision-making processes like DAOs, should be included to establish trust.

The roadmap outlines the project's development timeline, ensuring investors and the community understand the steps required to achieve key milestones. A roadmap typically starts with market research and team formation, followed by the development of smart contracts and testnet deployment. The next phases focus on fundraising through ICO, IDO, or IEO, token distribution, and liquidity provisioning on exchanges. After the initial launch, the project progresses towards exchange listings, beta platform releases, partnerships, and eventual full-scale adoption. Long-term development goals such as interoperability, cross-chain functionality, scalability improvements, and further decentralization should be included to demonstrate the project's growth vision.

A well-prepared whitepaper and roadmap improve transparency, attract investors, and provide a structured execution plan. They serve as living documents that evolve as the project progresses, ensuring alignment between the development team, investors, and the broader blockchain community. By combining a technically sound whitepaper with a realistic and strategic roadmap, cryptocurrency projects can build credibility and ensure long-term sustainability.

Token Allocation and Vesting Schedules

Token allocation and vesting schedules are critical components of a cryptocurrency project's tokenomics, ensuring fair distribution, preventing market manipulation, and promoting long-term stability. A well-structured allocation model defines how tokens are distributed among different stakeholders, including the development team, early investors, community participants, and ecosystem incentives. Proper vesting schedules prevent immediate sell-offs by locking tokens for a specific period, ensuring that key contributors remain committed to the project's growth.

Token allocation typically follows a structured breakdown to balance fairness, liquidity, and incentives. Common allocation categories include a percentage for the public sale or initial offering, often ranging from 20% to 40% of the total supply, ensuring that retail investors and early adopters have access to the token. A portion is reserved for the founding team, typically between 10% and 20%, ensuring that developers and executives remain incentivized to continue building the project. Strategic investors, venture capital firms, and private sale participants usually receive 10% to 30% of the supply, providing early funding to support the project's development and marketing efforts. Community rewards, staking incentives, liquidity mining, and ecosystem development often receive around 20% to 30%, fostering network participation and growth. Lastly, a reserve fund or treasury allocation, ranging from 5% to 15%, ensures that the project has the necessary capital for future expansions, partnerships, and unforeseen challenges.

Vesting schedules are essential for preventing token dumping, which can destabilize prices and erode investor confidence. Tokens allocated to team members and advisors typically follow a multi-year vesting schedule, preventing them from selling their holdings immediately. A common approach includes a cliff period, often lasting six to twelve months, during which no tokens are released. After the cliff period, gradual linear vesting distributes tokens in small portions over the following months or years. For example, a team allocation with a four-year vesting schedule might release 25% of tokens each year to ensure long-term commitment.

Private sale investors and early backers often have shorter vesting periods, such as 6 to 18 months, to balance liquidity with project stability. Public sale participants may receive their tokens immediately or have a small vesting period to prevent excessive price volatility. Community incentives and staking rewards are typically released based on usage and participation over time rather than all at once.

Well-structured token allocations and vesting schedules build trust, prevent price manipulation, and encourage sustainable ecosystem growth. Projects that fail to implement vesting mechanisms often suffer from early investor sell-offs, leading to extreme volatility and a loss of confidence. By aligning token distribution with long-term development milestones, blockchain projects can ensure a fair and well-balanced economic model that supports steady adoption and market stability.

Marketing Strategies for a Successful Launch

Marketing strategies play a crucial role in the successful launch of a cryptocurrency project, ensuring that it gains visibility, attracts investors, and builds a strong community. A well-planned marketing campaign should create awareness, establish credibility, and generate demand before and after the token launch. Given the highly competitive nature of the crypto space, strategic positioning, targeted promotions, and community-driven engagement are essential for sustained growth and adoption.

A strong brand identity is the foundation of an effective marketing strategy. This includes a professional logo, a well-designed website, a compelling whitepaper, and a clear, engaging narrative that highlights the project's value proposition. A well-crafted story differentiates the project from competitors and makes it easier for potential investors and users to understand its benefits. The website should be optimized for SEO and feature essential information such as the roadmap, tokenomics, team details, partnerships, and links to relevant social channels.

Community engagement is one of the most critical elements of crypto marketing. Building an active and loyal community on platforms like Telegram, Discord, and Twitter fosters organic discussions, increases trust, and helps spread the word about the project. Hosting AMA (Ask Me Anything) sessions with founders and developers encourages transparency and allows potential investors to ask questions directly. Incentivizing engagement through airdrops, referral programs, and staking rewards encourages more people to participate and spread awareness.

Social media marketing is vital for establishing a presence in the crypto industry. Twitter is one of the most active platforms for crypto discussions, making it an essential tool for sharing updates, partnerships, and industry insights. LinkedIn and Medium are useful for publishing in-depth articles and thought leadership pieces, while Reddit and Bitcointalk forums help engage with a broader crypto audience. Short-form video content on platforms like YouTube and TikTok can also enhance visibility and attract a younger demographic interested in blockchain technology.

Influencer marketing has proven to be highly effective in the crypto space. Partnering with crypto influencers, analysts, and YouTubers with large followings can help projects reach a wider audience. Selecting reputable influencers who align with the project's vision ensures credibility and minimizes the risk of associating with speculative promoters. Paid collaborations, sponsored reviews, and organic mentions can drive significant interest leading up to the token launch.

PR and media outreach help build credibility and attract institutional investors. Press releases in major crypto and finance publications such as CoinDesk, CoinTelegraph, Decrypt, and Bloomberg increase legitimacy and provide valuable exposure. Guest appearances on industry podcasts, webinars, and blockchain events help project leaders showcase their expertise and vision to a broader audience.

Paid advertising and PPC campaigns through platforms like Google Ads, Twitter Ads, and crypto-specific ad networks can be effective in driving traffic to the project's website. However, some mainstream platforms have restrictions on crypto-related ads, requiring careful planning and adherence to policies. Display ads on crypto news sites, banner ads on community forums, and native advertising through crypto newsletters are alternative strategies that offer targeted visibility.

Exchange listings and launchpad partnerships significantly impact a project's success. Getting listed on major centralized exchanges (CEXs) like Binance, Coinbase, and Kraken enhances credibility and liquidity. Participating in launchpads such as Binance Launchpad, Polkastarter, and DAO Maker provides early exposure and access to a dedicated investor base. Strong exchange partnerships also improve token accessibility, making it easier for users to trade and invest.

Gamification and viral marketing tactics can drive engagement and growth. Creating NFT drops, staking challenges, trading competitions, and referral contests helps incentivize community participation. Hosting blockchain hackathons, bounty programs, and DeFi integration incentives further encourage adoption among developers and users.

Regulatory compliance and transparency build investor trust. Clear legal disclaimers, terms of service, and KYC/AML compliance ensure that the project operates within legal frameworks. Conducting third-party smart contract audits and security assessments enhances credibility and reassures investors of the project's legitimacy.

A well-executed marketing strategy integrates brand positioning, community engagement, social media, influencer partnerships, PR outreach, paid advertising, exchange listings, and compliance to maximize visibility and trust. By combining organic growth with strategic promotional efforts, cryptocurrency projects can successfully attract investors, sustain momentum, and establish a strong presence in the market.

Chapter 8
Listing Your Coin on Exchanges

Listing a cryptocurrency on exchanges is a crucial step in ensuring liquidity, accessibility, and broader market adoption. A well-planned exchange listing strategy enhances visibility, attracts investors, and facilitates trading. Crypto exchanges are categorized into centralized exchanges (CEXs) and decentralized exchanges (DEXs), each with distinct listing processes, requirements, and benefits.

Before applying for a listing, a project must ensure that its token meets the necessary technical, security, and regulatory standards. The token should comply with blockchain-specific protocols such as ERC-20 (Ethereum), BEP-20 (Binance Smart Chain), or SPL (Solana) for compatibility with wallets and smart contracts. Conducting a smart contract audit by reputable firms like CertiK, OpenZeppelin, or PeckShield increases trust and prevents security vulnerabilities that could lead to hacks or exploits.

Listing on a centralized exchange (CEX) involves a formal application process where the project submits details such as the whitepaper, tokenomics, roadmap, team background, liquidity provisions, and compliance measures. Large exchanges like Binance, Coinbase, Kraken, and KuCoin require projects to demonstrate strong market demand, an active user base, and regulatory compliance. Exchange listing fees vary, with some top-tier exchanges charging significant amounts, ranging from $100,000 to several million dollars, depending on the project's valuation and liquidity requirements. In return, a CEX provides a trusted trading environment, advanced trading tools, fiat on-ramps, and increased liquidity.

Mid-tier exchanges such as Gate.io, Huobi, MEXC, and OKX offer more accessible listing opportunities for new projects. These platforms have lower listing fees and may accept emerging projects with strong communities. Some exchanges allow IEOs (Initial Exchange Offerings), where tokens are sold directly through the exchange, providing early liquidity and visibility.

For projects focusing on decentralization, listing on decentralized exchanges (DEXs) such as Uniswap, PancakeSwap, SushiSwap, and Raydium is essential. DEX listings require no formal approval process, as they operate on automated market maker (AMM) protocols that enable instant token trading through liquidity pools. To list on a DEX, a project must provide liquidity by pairing its token with popular assets like ETH, BNB, or USDT, ensuring smooth trading. Projects can use launchpads like Polkastarter, DAO Maker, or TrustSwap to increase exposure before listing.

Liquidity is a key factor in exchange listings. Low liquidity results in high price slippage, discouraging investors and traders. To prevent this, projects must allocate funds for market-making services, ensuring there are enough buy and sell orders to facilitate stable trading. Liquidity incentives, such as staking and yield farming rewards, attract users and increase token adoption.

Marketing and community engagement are vital before and after listing. A successful listing announcement across social media, press releases, and crypto news platforms like CoinDesk, CoinTelegraph, and Decrypt generates excitement and trading activity. Coordinating with crypto influencers, YouTubers, and Telegram communities boosts visibility. Hosting trading competitions, airdrops, and exchange AMA sessions encourages user participation and liquidity growth.

Regulatory compliance is another critical aspect of exchange listings. Projects must ensure they adhere to Know Your Customer (KYC), Anti-Money Laundering (AML), and securities laws in different jurisdictions. Exchanges often require proof of legal compliance to mitigate risks. Some projects seek legal opinions and licensing before applying for listings on regulated platforms.

After listing, continuous market monitoring and liquidity management are necessary to maintain stable trading conditions. Engaging with the exchange's market-making partners helps prevent price manipulation and ensures smooth order execution. Regular updates, community interactions, and partnerships contribute to sustained trading volume and investor confidence.

By implementing a strategic CEX and DEX listing approach, ensuring strong liquidity, compliance, and marketing efforts, and maintaining an active post-listing engagement strategy, cryptocurrency projects can maximize adoption, improve token utility, and achieve long-term market success.

Understanding the Exchange Listing Process

Understanding the exchange listing process is crucial for successfully launching and trading a cryptocurrency on centralized exchanges (CEXs) and decentralized exchanges (DEXs). A well-planned listing strategy increases liquidity, improves accessibility, and enhances the token's credibility. The listing process involves several steps, including application submission, due diligence, liquidity provisioning, and marketing efforts to maximize trading volume and investor interest.

The first step in listing a token on a centralized exchange (CEX) is submitting an application form on the exchange's official listing page. Top exchanges such as Binance, Coinbase, Kraken, and OKX have strict requirements and conduct thorough due diligence before approving tokens. The application typically includes details on the project's whitepaper, tokenomics, team members, technical architecture, liquidity strategy, and security measures. Exchanges assess a token's market demand, trading volume potential, legal compliance, and real-world utility to determine eligibility.

If the application meets the exchange's standards, the project undergoes a security audit to ensure that the smart contract is free from vulnerabilities. Exchanges often require third-party security audits from firms like CertiK, OpenZeppelin, or PeckShield to verify the contract's integrity and prevent exploits. In some cases, exchanges request additional documentation, such as proof of regulatory compliance, financial statements, or KYC/AML policies.

After passing due diligence, the next step is negotiating listing fees and liquidity requirements. High-tier exchanges may charge between $100,000 to several million dollars for listings, while mid-tier exchanges have lower fees. Some exchanges offer free listings for promising projects that align with their ecosystem. Projects must also commit to liquidity provisioning, ensuring that enough tokens and trading pairs (e.g., USDT, BTC, ETH) are available to prevent price volatility. Many projects partner with market-making firms to provide sufficient liquidity and maintain smooth order book activity.

For decentralized exchanges (DEXs) like Uniswap, PancakeSwap, SushiSwap, and Raydium, the listing process is more straightforward. Unlike CEXs, DEXs operate on automated market maker (AMM) protocols, allowing projects to list their tokens permissionlessly by creating liquidity pools. Projects must pair their token with stablecoins or popular assets such as ETH or BNB and provide an initial liquidity amount to facilitate trading. To gain visibility, projects often launch Initial DEX Offerings (IDOs) on platforms like Polkastarter, DAO Maker, or TrustSwap, attracting investors before the token is available for trading.

Marketing and community engagement play a critical role in a successful exchange listing. Before and after the listing, projects should conduct press releases, social media campaigns, influencer partnerships, and exchange AMA sessions to generate excitement. Listings should be announced on crypto news platforms like CoinDesk, CoinTelegraph, and Decrypt to reach a broader audience. To increase adoption, many projects incentivize liquidity providers with staking rewards, airdrops, and trading competitions on the exchange.

After listing, continuous market monitoring and liquidity management ensure that trading remains stable. Projects should track trading volume, order book depth, and price movements, making necessary adjustments to prevent manipulation and excessive volatility. Engaging with the exchange's market-making services and liquidity providers helps maintain a healthy trading environment.

Regulatory compliance is also a crucial factor, as different exchanges operate under specific legal frameworks. Some exchanges require legal opinions and adherence to securities laws, particularly in regulated jurisdictions like the U.S. and Europe. Ensuring compliance with KYC (Know Your Customer) and AML (Anti-Money

Laundering) requirements can prevent delisting or legal issues in the future.

By understanding the exchange listing process, preparing strong liquidity management strategies, ensuring compliance, and executing marketing campaigns, projects can maximize their token's success and establish long-term credibility in the cryptocurrency market.

Centralized vs. Decentralized Exchanges (CEX vs. DEX)

Centralized and decentralized exchanges (CEX vs. DEX) are the two primary platforms for trading cryptocurrencies, each offering distinct advantages and trade-offs in terms of security, liquidity, accessibility, and user control. Understanding their differences is essential for both cryptocurrency projects looking to list tokens and investors seeking the best trading experience.

Centralized exchanges (CEXs) are managed by a central authority that facilitates the buying, selling, and custody of cryptocurrencies. Platforms like Binance, Coinbase, Kraken, and KuCoin operate under a structured framework, providing high liquidity, fast transactions, and advanced trading features such as limit orders, futures, margin trading, and fiat on-ramps. Since CEXs manage users' funds, they offer custodial wallets, meaning users do not directly control their private keys. While this simplifies the trading experience and enhances security through insured accounts, it also introduces a single point of failure, making CEXs vulnerable to hacking, regulatory restrictions, and operational risks.

Decentralized exchanges (DEXs), such as Uniswap, PancakeSwap, SushiSwap, and Curve Finance, operate on blockchain-based smart contracts and do not rely on intermediaries. Instead of order books, DEXs use automated market makers (AMMs), allowing users to trade directly from their wallets through liquidity pools. Since transactions occur on-chain, DEXs offer higher security and anonymity, as users maintain full control over their private keys and assets. However, DEXs often suffer from lower liquidity, higher price slippage, and slower transaction speeds, especially on congested blockchains like Ethereum.

One of the key differences between CEXs and DEXs is regulatory oversight. CEXs must comply with Know Your Customer (KYC) and Anti-Money Laundering (AML) regulations, requiring users to verify their identities. This compliance ensures greater security and investor protection but limits accessibility for those who prioritize privacy. DEXs, on the other hand, operate in a permissionless manner, meaning users can trade without registration or identity verification. While this enhances decentralization, it also increases the risk of fraud, rug pulls, and illicit activities.

Liquidity is another major factor distinguishing CEXs from DEXs. Centralized exchanges offer deep liquidity pools and tighter spreads, allowing for faster execution of large trades with minimal price impact. DEXs rely on user-supplied liquidity, meaning trading volumes and slippage depend on the number of liquidity providers in a given pool. Impermanent loss is a common issue in DEXs, where liquidity providers may lose value compared to simply holding their assets due to price fluctuations in the pool.

Security considerations vary between the two models. While CEXs implement high-level security measures, such as cold storage, insurance funds, and regulatory compliance, they are prime targets for hacks, exchange shutdowns, and asset seizures. DEXs, being non-custodial, reduce counterparty risk but are susceptible to smart contract vulnerabilities, front-running attacks, and liquidity crises.

Proper smart contract audits and decentralized governance mechanisms help mitigate these risks in DEX environments.

User experience and accessibility also differ significantly. CEXs provide user-friendly interfaces, customer support, and fiat gateways, making them ideal for beginners and institutional traders. DEXs require users to interact with blockchain wallets (e.g., MetaMask, Trust Wallet) and pay gas fees, making them less intuitive for mainstream adoption. However, with the rise of Layer-2 solutions, cross-chain interoperability, and improved DEX UI/UX, decentralized exchanges are becoming more accessible.

For cryptocurrency projects looking to list tokens, CEXs offer greater exposure, market credibility, and guaranteed liquidity, but they often require high listing fees, compliance procedures, and ongoing engagement with exchange operators. DEX listings are permissionless, faster, and cheaper, but require strong liquidity incentives and community-driven market-making strategies to maintain trading volume and price stability.

Both centralized and decentralized exchanges play a crucial role in the crypto ecosystem. CEXs provide regulation, deep liquidity, and ease of use, making them essential for institutional adoption and mainstream investors. DEXs enable true decentralization, security, and financial sovereignty, catering to users who prioritize trustless trading and asset control. As the industry evolves, hybrid models incorporating CEX liquidity with DEX transparency may bridge the gap, offering the best of both worlds.

Liquidity and Market Making Strategies

Liquidity and market-making strategies are essential for ensuring a smooth trading experience, minimizing price volatility, and maintaining investor confidence in a cryptocurrency. Liquidity refers to the ease with which a token can be bought or sold without significantly impacting its price. A well-structured liquidity strategy improves price stability, attracts traders, and enhances the credibility of a project. Market making involves providing continuous buy and sell orders to maintain liquidity, narrow bid-ask spreads, and prevent drastic price swings.

For centralized exchanges (CEXs), liquidity is typically managed through an order book system, where traders place limit and market orders. High liquidity results in tight bid-ask spreads, reducing slippage and ensuring efficient price discovery. Projects listing on CEXs often partner with market-making firms such as GSR, Wintermute, or Jump Trading to maintain active trading volumes. Market makers provide continuous buy and sell orders at various price levels, preventing order book gaps and reducing volatility. Some exchanges require projects to commit a portion of their funds to liquidity provisioning or offer liquidity incentives in the form of rebates.

For decentralized exchanges (DEXs), liquidity is provided through automated market maker (AMM) models, where users supply liquidity to liquidity pools. Liquidity pools function by pairing tokens with assets such as ETH, BNB, or USDT in smart contract-based pools. Users who contribute liquidity earn a portion of the trading fees generated from swaps but face the risk of impermanent loss, which occurs when the price of the provided assets fluctuates. Popular DEX liquidity models include Uniswap's constant product model ($x * y = k$) and Balancer's multi-token AMM model, which allows flexible weight distributions.

Effective liquidity strategies involve initial liquidity provisioning, where a project allocates funds to bootstrap liquidity pools or provide market-making capital. Many projects conduct liquidity bootstrapping pools (LBPs) on platforms like Balancer and Copper, allowing dynamic price discovery while preventing price manipulation. Liquidity mining programs incentivize users to provide liquidity by offering governance tokens or staking rewards in return for their contributions.

Cross-exchange arbitrage opportunities also influence liquidity. When a token is listed on both CEXs and DEXs, price discrepancies between platforms create arbitrage opportunities, where traders buy from the lower-priced exchange and sell on the higher-priced one. Ensuring consistent liquidity across exchanges reduces price gaps and improves trading efficiency.

To further enhance liquidity, projects can establish token utility and real-world use cases, increasing demand and reducing speculative volatility. Ensuring that the token is integrated into DeFi platforms, staking protocols, payment networks, and governance mechanisms encourages long-term holding rather than short-term selling.

A well-structured liquidity and market-making strategy balances liquidity depth, trading volume, and incentives to sustain an active trading environment. By combining CEX liquidity partnerships, DEX liquidity pools, arbitrage-friendly structures, and incentive-driven programs, projects can create a healthy, stable, and liquid market that fosters long-term adoption and investor confidence.

Compliance and KYC/AML Considerations

Compliance with Know Your Customer (KYC) and Anti-Money Laundering (AML) regulations is essential for cryptocurrency projects, particularly those planning an Initial Coin Offering (ICO), Initial Exchange Offering (IEO), or Initial DEX Offering (IDO). These regulations help prevent financial crimes, protect investors, and ensure that projects operate within legal frameworks. Failure to comply with these requirements can result in regulatory penalties, exchange delistings, or restrictions on project operations in certain jurisdictions.

KYC regulations require projects to verify the identity of their investors and users before they can participate in token sales, staking, or financial services. This process typically involves collecting personal identification data, such as government-issued IDs, proof of residence, and biometric verification. Many projects integrate third-party KYC providers like Sumsub, Onfido, or IdentityMind to streamline the verification process and ensure compliance with data protection laws such as GDPR and CCPA. Exchanges, both centralized and decentralized, often enforce KYC policies to prevent fraud, identity theft, and unauthorized access.

AML measures focus on detecting and preventing illicit financial activities, such as money laundering and terrorist financing. Projects must implement risk-based monitoring systems that flag suspicious transactions, such as large fund transfers, rapid trading activity, or unusual withdrawal patterns. Blockchain analytics firms like Chainalysis, CipherTrace, and Elliptic help identify illicit activities by tracing wallet addresses linked to blacklisted entities. AML programs also require businesses to report suspicious activities to regulatory authorities like FinCEN (U.S.), FCA (UK), or MAS (Singapore).

For token projects listing on centralized exchanges (CEXs), compliance is a critical requirement. Most regulated exchanges, such as Binance, Coinbase, and Kraken, require projects to submit legal documentation proving that they adhere to KYC/AML laws. This includes legal opinions on token classification (security vs. utility token), corporate registrations, and financial disclosures. Projects that fail to meet compliance standards may face delisting risks, regulatory investigations, or investor lawsuits.

Decentralized exchanges (DEXs), which operate on smart contract-based liquidity pools, historically did not enforce KYC/AML policies. However, due to increasing regulatory scrutiny, some regulated DEXs, such as dYdX and Uniswap, have started implementing compliance measures, including geo-restrictions and wallet blacklisting for high-risk jurisdictions.

Crypto projects must also consider international compliance regulations, as different countries have varying legal frameworks. The European Union's MiCA (Markets in Crypto-Assets) Regulation, the U.S. SEC's classification of tokens as securities, and Asia's stricter licensing requirements impact how projects operate globally. Many projects establish legal entities in crypto-friendly jurisdictions such as Switzerland, Singapore, or the Cayman Islands to navigate regulatory complexities while remaining compliant.

Smart contract audits and transparent governance structures enhance compliance efforts. By implementing decentralized autonomous organizations (DAOs), multi-signature treasury wallets, and transparent fund allocation reports, projects can demonstrate ethical business practices and investor protection.

A strong compliance and KYC/AML framework ensures long-term project sustainability, investor trust, and regulatory approval. By integrating identity verification, risk monitoring, legal structuring, and transparent governance, crypto projects can minimize legal risks while fostering global adoption in a rapidly evolving regulatory landscape.

Chapter 9
Building a Crypto Community

Building a strong crypto community is essential for the success and long-term sustainability of a cryptocurrency project. A vibrant and engaged community drives adoption, increases awareness, and establishes trust among investors, developers, and users. The crypto space thrives on network effects, where an active user base contributes to liquidity, trading volume, and ecosystem growth. A well-structured community strategy enhances credibility, fosters innovation, and helps projects withstand market fluctuations.

The first step in community building is defining a clear vision and value proposition. Crypto users are drawn to projects with a strong mission, whether it's decentralization, financial inclusion, or blockchain innovation. Communicating the project's goals, token utility, roadmap, and governance model helps attract like-minded participants. Transparency in decision-making, frequent updates, and responsiveness to feedback are key factors in maintaining trust and engagement.

Social media and communication channels play a crucial role in community development. Platforms like Twitter, Telegram, Discord, and Reddit serve as hubs for discussions, updates, and announcements. Twitter is essential for broad engagement, allowing projects to share news, partnerships, and industry insights. Telegram and Discord provide real-time interaction, AMAs (Ask Me Anything) sessions, and developer discussions. Reddit fosters long-form discussions, while YouTube and TikTok help with educational content and visual storytelling. Consistent content marketing, including blog posts on Medium and LinkedIn, enhances credibility and attracts both technical and non-technical audiences.

Incentivizing community participation accelerates growth and engagement. Airdrops, staking rewards, referral programs, and gamification encourage users to become active participants in the ecosystem. Liquidity mining, yield farming, and governance incentives attract DeFi users, while NFT drops and exclusive memberships appeal to Web3 enthusiasts. Well-structured ambassador programs allow passionate community members to represent the project, creating grassroots advocacy.

Partnerships and collaborations with other blockchain projects, influencers, and media outlets expand reach and credibility. Engaging with crypto influencers, YouTubers, and industry analysts increases visibility. Strategic partnerships with DeFi protocols, metaverse projects, and DAOs integrate the token into broader ecosystems, driving real-world use cases. Listing on CoinMarketCap, CoinGecko, and top-tier exchanges enhances credibility and attracts investors.

Hosting virtual and in-person events strengthens community bonds. Webinars, AMAs, hackathons, and developer meetups provide direct engagement opportunities. Blockchain conferences, like ETHDenver, Binance Blockchain Week, and Token2049, offer networking opportunities with industry leaders. Community-driven events, such as trading competitions, NFT minting contests, and DAO voting sessions, keep users engaged.

Decentralized governance and community decision-making foster trust and long-term participation. DAOs enable token holders to propose, vote on, and implement changes in the project.

Governance tokens empower the community, making users feel valued and increasing their commitment to the ecosystem. Transparent governance mechanisms, such as multi-signature treasury management and on-chain voting, enhance credibility and decentralization.

Maintaining a safe and positive environment within the community is crucial. Strong moderation, clear guidelines, and anti-spam measures ensure a constructive space for discussions. Addressing scams, phishing attempts, and FUD (fear, uncertainty, doubt) proactively helps protect the community from misinformation and security threats.

Sustaining long-term engagement requires continuous innovation and adaptability. Regular updates, new product launches, and ecosystem expansions keep the community excited and invested. Actively listening to user feedback, implementing feature requests, and responding to concerns strengthen relationships between the project team and its supporters.

A successful crypto community thrives on transparency, engagement, incentives, and decentralization. By leveraging social media, strategic partnerships, governance models, and innovative rewards, blockchain projects can cultivate a loyal, engaged, and self-sustaining ecosystem that supports long-term adoption and market growth.

Engaging with Developers and Investors

Engaging with developers and investors is critical for the long-term success of a cryptocurrency project. Developers drive innovation, build applications on the ecosystem, and ensure the project's technical robustness, while investors provide financial backing and liquidity. A well-structured engagement strategy strengthens both groups' commitment, fosters growth, and enhances credibility.

To attract developers, a project must provide a developer-friendly environment with well-documented APIs, SDKs, and open-source resources. Hosting a GitHub repository with clean, modular, and well-commented code allows contributors to audit, improve, and build on the project. Offering technical documentation, tutorials, and developer guides ensures that onboarding is seamless. Platforms like Ethereum, Solana, and Polkadot have succeeded by maintaining strong developer portals and hackathons, encouraging innovation and ecosystem expansion.

Organizing developer engagement programs such as hackathons, coding challenges, and grant programs incentivizes technical contributions. Offering bug bounties and security audits through platforms like Immunefi helps improve the project’s resilience while rewarding developers for finding vulnerabilities. Developer AMAs, workshops, and webinars provide direct communication channels between the project team and builders, fostering collaboration.

Developers are also drawn to ecosystem incentives, such as developer funds, staking rewards, and grants for building dApps, smart contracts, or cross-chain integrations. Projects like Binance Smart Chain, Avalanche, and Polygon have established multimillion-dollar developer funds to attract talent. Offering gas fee subsidies, infrastructure support, and DAO governance opportunities encourages long-term commitment from the developer community.

Investor engagement requires clear communication, transparency, and strategic relationship management. Institutional investors and venture capital (VC) firms seek strong tokenomics, liquidity structures, and compliance measures before committing capital. A well-crafted pitch deck and investor brief outlining market potential, competitive advantages, and financial projections is essential when approaching VCs and angel investors.

For retail investors, active community engagement and transparency build trust. Hosting regular investor updates, tokenomics breakdowns, and roadmap milestones reassures token holders about the project's long-term vision. Earning trust through transparent governance—such as DAO voting, multi-signature wallet treasury management, and open-source financial disclosures—encourages long-term holding instead of speculative trading.

Building relationships with crypto influencers, institutional funds, and launchpads increases investor confidence. Launching an IDO (Initial DEX Offering) on platforms like Polkastarter or DAO Maker, or an IEO (Initial Exchange Offering) on Binance Launchpad, ensures structured fundraising with immediate exchange listings. Tokenomics models that incorporate vesting schedules, staking rewards, and deflationary mechanisms attract long-term investors rather than short-term speculators.

Maintaining strong liquidity and exchange support is essential for investor engagement. High liquidity reduces slippage and enhances trading efficiency, encouraging large-scale investors to participate. Partnering with market makers and liquidity providers ensures smooth trading on centralized and decentralized exchanges.

Both developers and investors require ongoing engagement. Developer conferences, whitepaper revisions, roadmap adjustments, and technical support keep developers involved. For investors, regular AMAs, earnings reports, and community-driven initiatives help sustain interest and long-term participation.

By bridging technical innovation with financial backing, crypto projects can attract top-tier developers and committed investors, ensuring sustained growth, adoption, and long-term success.

Social Media, Forums, and PR Strategies

Social media, forums, and PR strategies play a crucial role in the success of a cryptocurrency project by driving awareness, fostering engagement, and establishing credibility. A well-executed marketing campaign leverages multiple digital channels to attract investors, developers, and users while maintaining transparency and trust. Given the competitive nature of the crypto space, projects must implement an integrated approach that combines social media presence, active forum participation, and strategic PR initiatives.

Social media platforms serve as the primary channels for engagement, announcements, and community-building. Twitter (X) is one of the most active spaces for crypto discussions, where projects share updates, partnerships, market trends, and educational threads. Regular posting, interactive Q&As, and participation in industry trends ensure visibility. Telegram and Discord are essential for real-time community interaction, providing users with direct communication channels for AMAs (Ask Me Anything), support, and discussions on project developments. YouTube and TikTok are effective for visual storytelling, offering explainer videos, live streams, and short-form educational content to reach a broader audience.

Crypto forums and discussion boards are valuable for credibility and organic outreach. Platforms like Reddit (r/cryptocurrency, r/ethtrader, r/defi), BitcoinTalk, and Stack Exchange facilitate long-form discussions, helping projects establish thought leadership. Engaging with these communities through project updates, answering technical questions, and contributing to discussions enhances reputation and trust. Medium and Substack provide a space for publishing deep-dive articles, technical papers, and research-driven insights that appeal to developers and institutional investors.

Public relations (PR) strategies focus on securing media coverage, building industry authority, and managing reputational risks. Getting featured on top-tier crypto news outlets such as CoinDesk, CoinTelegraph, Decrypt, and The Block boosts visibility and credibility. Press releases announcing partnerships, token listings, funding rounds, and milestone achievements ensure media traction. Guest appearances on blockchain podcasts, YouTube interviews with industry influencers, and keynote speeches at blockchain events establish project leaders as experts in the field.

Influencer marketing remains a powerful tool in crypto promotion. Collaborating with reputable crypto influencers, YouTubers, and analysts increases reach and trust. Choosing influencers who align with the project's vision and have engaged communities is key to avoiding low-quality promotions. Partnering with industry experts for research-backed reports and technical reviews strengthens credibility among institutional investors and developers.

Community-driven engagement strategies further amplify reach. Hosting giveaways, referral programs, staking incentives, and NFT drops incentivizes participation. Running viral marketing campaigns such as meme contests, interactive polls, and bounty programs attracts organic traffic. Engaging with DeFi, GameFi, and Web3 communities by integrating the token into existing ecosystems expands the user base.

Crisis management and reputation handling are crucial in crypto PR. Addressing negative press, clarifying misinformation, and maintaining transparency during market volatility prevent FUD (fear, uncertainty, and doubt) from damaging the project's credibility. Rapid response teams for handling security incidents, regulatory scrutiny, and investor concerns strengthen community trust.

A well-rounded marketing strategy combines social media consistency, active forum engagement, PR-driven credibility, and influencer collaborations. By integrating multiple channels, fostering transparency, and maintaining a strong digital presence, crypto projects can maximize visibility, attract investors and developers, and ensure sustained adoption in a competitive market.

Partnerships and Collaborations in the Crypto Space

Partnerships and collaborations in the crypto space play a vital role in expanding a project's ecosystem, increasing adoption, and enhancing credibility. Strategic alliances with blockchain projects, DeFi platforms, institutional investors, and industry leaders create new opportunities for growth while fostering innovation and market integration. Successful partnerships help projects reach wider audiences, strengthen liquidity, and improve technological capabilities.

One of the most effective forms of partnerships is exchange collaborations, where projects work with centralized exchanges (CEXs) like Binance, Coinbase, Kraken, and KuCoin to list their tokens. These partnerships provide increased liquidity, exposure to new investors, and access to fiat on-ramps. Decentralized exchanges (DEXs) such as Uniswap, PancakeSwap, and SushiSwap also offer liquidity partnerships where projects provide incentives for users to supply liquidity through farming and staking rewards.

Blockchain infrastructure collaborations are essential for enhancing scalability, security, and interoperability. Projects often integrate with Layer-1 blockchains like Ethereum, Solana, BNB Chain, and Avalanche to build dApps, while Layer-2 solutions such as Polygon, Arbitrum, and Optimism help reduce transaction costs and improve efficiency. Partnerships with cross-chain bridges like Wormhole, Synapse, and Stargate allow assets to move seamlessly between different blockchains, increasing utility and adoption.

DeFi partnerships strengthen financial services by integrating with lending platforms, liquidity providers, and yield farming protocols. Projects often collaborate with DeFi platforms like Aave, Compound, Curve Finance, and Yearn Finance to offer staking rewards, lending options, and governance integrations. Liquidity partnerships with market-making firms such as Jump Trading, Wintermute, and GSR ensure price stability and reduced slippage for token trading.

Institutional collaborations with venture capital firms, hedge funds, and Web3 investment funds provide funding and strategic guidance. Crypto VCs such as Andreessen Horowitz (a16z), Paradigm, Sequoia Capital, and Alameda Research help projects scale through capital injections, industry connections, and mentorship. These partnerships also boost credibility, making projects more attractive to retail and institutional investors.

NFT and gaming collaborations expand token utility by integrating with GameFi, play-to-earn (P2E), and metaverse platforms. Projects often partner with leading NFT marketplaces such as OpenSea, Rarible, and Magic Eden to launch exclusive collections, while GameFi integrations with Axie Infinity, Gala Games, and The Sandbox enable tokenized assets and in-game rewards. Strategic alliances with esports teams and influencers further increase visibility in the gaming community.

Regulatory and compliance partnerships help crypto projects navigate legal frameworks and ensure long-term viability. Collaborating with blockchain analytics firms like Chainalysis, Elliptic, and CipherTrace assists with KYC/AML compliance and fraud prevention. Legal partnerships with crypto law firms help projects register in crypto-friendly jurisdictions like Switzerland, Singapore, and the Cayman Islands while ensuring adherence to evolving regulatory requirements.

Marketing and influencer collaborations are key to expanding brand awareness and user acquisition. Partnering with crypto influencers, YouTubers, and Twitter (X) analysts increases exposure to retail investors. Collaborations with media outlets such as CoinDesk, CoinTelegraph, and Decrypt generate industry recognition through press releases, sponsored content, and interviews.

DAO and governance collaborations empower decentralized decision-making by integrating with multi-signature wallets, on-chain voting systems, and treasury management platforms. Partnerships with governance solutions like Snapshot, Aragon, and Gnosis Safe ensure transparent community-driven project management.

Strategic partnerships in the crypto space drive innovation, expand adoption, and establish credibility. By collaborating with exchanges, blockchain infrastructure providers, DeFi protocols, VCs, NFT platforms, regulatory firms, and influencers, projects can position themselves for long-term success. A strong partnership network enhances liquidity, increases token utility, and strengthens ecosystem development, ensuring sustainable growth in an increasingly competitive market.

Handling Community Concerns and Technical Support

Handling community concerns and providing effective technical support are critical for maintaining trust, engagement, and long-term success in the cryptocurrency space. The decentralized nature of blockchain projects means that users, developers, and investors rely on transparent communication, swift issue resolution, and proactive support mechanisms to ensure smooth operations. A well-structured community support strategy enhances user experience, prevents misinformation, and strengthens loyalty.

The first step in addressing community concerns is establishing transparent and open communication channels. Platforms such as Telegram, Discord, Twitter (X), Reddit, and Medium serve as primary touchpoints for users to ask questions, report issues, and discuss the project. Maintaining an official blog, FAQ section, and help center provides structured information, reducing confusion and repetitive inquiries. Projects should ensure that official announcements are pinned and regularly updated to prevent FUD (fear, uncertainty, and doubt) from spreading.

Community concerns should be categorized into technical issues, security concerns, token-related inquiries, and general feedback. A dedicated support team, including moderators and developers, should monitor these concerns in real time, ensuring quick responses and escalation when necessary. Automated chatbots and AI-driven customer service tools can be integrated into support channels to handle common questions efficiently while allowing human intervention for complex issues.

Technical support requires a structured approach to troubleshooting and bug resolution. Maintaining a public issue tracker on GitHub or a support ticketing system enables developers to track and prioritize reported bugs, smart contract vulnerabilities, and UI/UX problems. For blockchain projects, gas fee issues, transaction failures, wallet integration errors, and liquidity concerns are common pain points that require well-documented solutions. Providing step-by-step guides, video tutorials, and developer documentation ensures that users can resolve minor issues independently.

Security concerns must be handled with urgency to protect community members and maintain project integrity. In the event of a smart contract exploit, phishing attack, or wallet vulnerability, projects must issue immediate alerts and take necessary actions such as pausing transactions, rolling out patches, or collaborating with blockchain security firms like CertiK, PeckShield, and SlowMist. Bug bounty programs incentivize ethical hackers to report vulnerabilities before they can be exploited.

Token-related inquiries, including listing updates, airdrop distribution, staking rewards, and vesting schedules, should be addressed through regular AMAs (Ask Me Anything), governance proposals, and official reports. Ensuring clarity in tokenomics, vesting timelines, and exchange listings prevents misinformation and enhances investor confidence.

Crisis management is an essential aspect of handling major community concerns. In cases of price volatility, sudden token dumps, regulatory scrutiny, or exchange delistings, the project team should issue well-structured statements, explain the situation transparently, and provide actionable solutions. Delays in response or lack of communication during crises can lead to panic selling and loss of trust.

Feedback collection and implementation are crucial for continuous improvement. Engaging with the community through polls, DAO governance votes, and feedback forms helps projects align with user needs. Integrating community-driven development ensures that valuable suggestions are incorporated into the roadmap, making users feel heard and valued.

A well-managed community support strategy strengthens project credibility, ensures smooth user experiences, and builds long-term engagement. By combining transparent communication, structured technical support, proactive security measures, and user-driven improvements, crypto projects can effectively manage concerns and establish a loyal, thriving ecosystem.

Chapter 10
Security and Compliance

Security and compliance are fundamental to the success and longevity of any cryptocurrency project. In an industry known for cyber threats, regulatory uncertainties, and financial risks, a well-structured security and compliance strategy ensures investor confidence, protects user funds, and aligns with global legal requirements. Blockchain projects must proactively address security vulnerabilities while adhering to legal frameworks to avoid regulatory scrutiny and maintain trust.

Security Measures

Robust security mechanisms prevent hacking attempts, smart contract exploits, and unauthorized access to user funds. Smart contract audits are critical for identifying vulnerabilities before deployment. Reputable security firms like CertiK, OpenZeppelin, PeckShield, and Trail of Bits conduct in-depth audits, analyzing contract code for potential exploits such as reentrancy attacks, integer overflows, front-running vulnerabilities, and privilege escalation flaws. Regular code reviews, formal verification, and penetration testing strengthen project security.

Blockchain networks must implement multi-layered security protocols, including end-to-end encryption, multi-signature wallets, and cold storage solutions for treasury management. Multi-signature wallets, such as Gnosis Safe, require multiple approvals before executing high-value transactions, reducing the risk of a single point of failure. For exchanges and wallet providers, integrating Hardware Security Modules (HSMs) ensures that private keys remain secure.

To protect users, projects should implement phishing protection mechanisms, domain verification, and scam prevention tools. Fraudulent websites and impersonation scams are common in crypto, making it essential to educate users on identifying suspicious activities and enabling two-factor authentication (2FA) for account security. Real-time monitoring tools, such as Chainalysis, Elliptic, and CipherTrace, help track fraudulent transactions, detect money laundering activities, and blacklist compromised wallet addresses.

Decentralized finance (DeFi) protocols face additional security risks, including flash loan attacks, oracle manipulation, and liquidity pool exploits. Implementing time-lock mechanisms, circuit breakers, and automated security alerts mitigates the impact of potential exploits. Decentralized exchanges (DEXs) should use decentralized price oracles (Chainlink, Band Protocol) and audited liquidity pool structures to prevent price manipulation attacks.

Compliance Considerations

Regulatory compliance ensures that cryptocurrency projects operate within legal boundaries, reducing the risk of penalties, lawsuits, or delistings from exchanges. Compliance requirements vary across jurisdictions, with countries like the U.S., EU, Singapore, and Switzerland imposing strict financial regulations on digital assets.

Know Your Customer (KYC) and Anti-Money Laundering (AML) requirements are critical for projects involved in fundraising, token sales, and exchange listings. Implementing KYC verification through providers like Sumsub, Onfido, or IdentityMind ensures that users are authenticated, preventing fraudulent activities and money laundering. Centralized exchanges (CEXs) must comply with Financial Action Task Force (FATF) travel rules, ensuring transaction traceability and reporting obligations.

For token launches, projects must determine whether their token qualifies as a security, utility, or governance token under financial regulations. The U.S. SEC's Howey Test helps classify tokens, where security tokens are subject to Securities and Exchange Commission (SEC) regulations and may require proper registrations or exemptions. Countries like Switzerland and Singapore offer crypto-friendly legal frameworks, making them ideal jurisdictions for blockchain startups.

DeFi projects and decentralized autonomous organizations (DAOs) must also navigate regulatory challenges. While DAOs operate without centralized control, some jurisdictions may classify them as legal entities responsible for governance decisions and financial compliance. Ensuring transparent governance, decentralized control, and smart contract-based decision-making reduces the risk of regulatory crackdowns.

Ensuring compliance with data protection laws such as GDPR (General Data Protection Regulation) and CCPA (California Consumer Privacy Act) is crucial for protecting user privacy. Projects handling personal data must implement secure storage, encryption, and access controls to prevent data breaches.

Security Incident Response and Crisis Management

In the event of a security breach, projects must have a well-defined incident response plan. A security response team, real-time monitoring tools, and automated emergency protocols can mitigate damages. If an exploit occurs, immediate actions such as pausing smart contract functions, notifying exchanges, and tracking stolen funds help contain the breach. Engaging with blockchain security firms and working with white-hat hackers through bug bounty programs prevents future attacks.

A comprehensive security and compliance strategy safeguards crypto projects from cyber threats, legal risks, and financial losses. By integrating smart contract audits, multi-layered security protocols, regulatory compliance measures, and incident response strategies, blockchain projects can maintain trust, protect assets, and ensure long-term sustainability in an evolving regulatory landscape. Prioritizing security and compliance not only mitigates risks but also positions the project for broader adoption and institutional investment.

Common Crypto Vulnerabilities and How to Prevent Them

Cryptocurrency projects face a wide range of security threats, including smart contract exploits, phishing attacks, wallet vulnerabilities, and exchange hacks. Cybercriminals often target blockchain networks, decentralized finance (DeFi) protocols, and crypto exchanges to steal funds, manipulate transactions, or disrupt services. Implementing robust security measures is essential to protect assets, maintain trust, and prevent catastrophic losses. Poorly written or unaudited smart contracts can contain critical security flaws that attackers exploit to steal funds or manipulate token balances. Reentrancy attacks allow hackers to drain funds before a contract updates its balance, while integer overflows and underflows create unexpected behaviors. Front-running attacks exploit pending transactions by submitting higher gas fees, and oracle manipulation distorts price feeds to execute fraudulent trades. These vulnerabilities can be mitigated by following secure coding practices, using reentrancy guards, implementing SafeMath libraries, relying on decentralized oracles, and undergoing rigorous smart contract audits by security firms like CertiK, OpenZeppelin, and PeckShield.

Centralized exchanges are prime targets for hacks due to the high volume of funds they manage. Hot wallet exploits occur when hackers gain access to exchange wallets, often leading to multimillion-dollar thefts. Insider trading and wash trading create artificial market activity and manipulate prices, while regulatory non-compliance can lead to lawsuits and delistings. Best practices for securing centralized exchanges include storing the majority of assets in cold wallets, using multi-signature authentication, integrating Hardware Security Modules (HSMs), and adhering to strict regulatory frameworks for Know Your Customer (KYC) and Anti-Money Laundering (AML) compliance. Implementing real-time monitoring and working with compliance firms like Chainalysis and CipherTrace helps detect suspicious transactions and prevent illicit financial activities.

Crypto wallets are also vulnerable to security threats, especially those involving private key exposure. Phishing attacks trick users into entering their private keys or seed phrases on fake wallet interfaces, while malware and keyloggers secretly capture sensitive information. Man-in-the-Middle (MITM) attacks intercept transactions between users and exchanges, altering the recipient address. Protecting crypto wallets requires the use of hardware wallets like Ledger and Trezor, enabling Two-Factor Authentication (2FA), verifying URLs before entering credentials, and avoiding downloading unverified software that could contain spyware. Air-gapped (offline) wallets provide additional security by keeping private keys completely disconnected from the internet.

DeFi platforms introduce new risks due to the complexity of smart contract interactions. Rug pulls and exit scams occur when project developers remove liquidity or mint excessive tokens, leaving investors with worthless assets. Flash loan attacks involve borrowing large amounts of funds without collateral and exploiting vulnerabilities in DeFi protocols. Governance exploits allow malicious actors to acquire large governance token holdings to manipulate protocol rules. These threats can be mitigated by verifying contract ownership, ensuring liquidity lock periods, implementing collateralized lending mechanisms, and decentralizing governance with time-locked decision-making processes.

Blockchain networks are also susceptible to 51% attacks, where an entity gains majority control of mining or staking power to execute double-spending attacks or halt network operations. This risk is especially high for smaller Proof of Work (PoW) blockchains with low hashrates. Implementing Proof of Stake (PoS) consensus mechanisms, chain checkpoints, and promoting decentralized mining pools can reduce the likelihood of such attacks.

Social engineering and fake airdrop scams are prevalent in the crypto space, where hackers impersonate official projects to trick users into signing malicious transactions or transferring funds to fraudulent addresses. Preventing these attacks requires community awareness campaigns, verification of official sources, and the use of smart contract whitelisting mechanisms to prevent unauthorized approvals.

Sybil attacks in DAOs and voting manipulation schemes create artificial influence over decentralized governance decisions. Attackers generate multiple fake identities or acquire large amounts of governance tokens to sway votes in their favor. Preventing these attacks requires stake-weighted voting, identity verification mechanisms, and decentralized governance models that limit the concentration of power.

Best practices for securing crypto projects include conducting regular security audits, using multi-signature cold storage wallets, following regulatory compliance guidelines, educating users about scams, and developing an incident response plan for potential breaches. Proactively monitoring the network for unusual activities, working with security firms, and offering bug bounties to ethical hackers can help identify vulnerabilities before they are exploited. Ensuring compliance with AML and KYC regulations protects the project from legal issues and enhances investor trust.

Crypto vulnerabilities pose serious risks, but a proactive security strategy can significantly reduce exposure to attacks. Implementing robust smart contract security, wallet protection mechanisms, regulatory compliance, and DeFi safeguards can prevent exploits, secure digital assets, and foster long-term trust in the ecosystem. By prioritizing security and transparency, blockchain projects can enhance legitimacy, prevent financial losses, and build a sustainable future in the cryptocurrency space.

Smart Contract Auditing and Security Best Practices

Smart contract auditing and security best practices are critical to ensuring the integrity, reliability, and security of blockchain-based applications. A vulnerable smart contract can lead to significant financial losses, exploits, and a loss of user trust. Given the immutable nature of blockchain, where deployed code cannot be changed without careful planning, identifying and mitigating security risks before deployment is crucial.

The first step in smart contract security is comprehensive code auditing, which involves a thorough review of the contract's logic, functions, and data structures. Common vulnerabilities include reentrancy attacks, where an attacker exploits recursive external calls before the contract updates its state, allowing funds to be drained. This can be mitigated by using checks-effects-interactions patterns, reentrancy guards, and ensuring that state changes occur before external calls. Integer overflows and underflows can result in unexpected arithmetic errors, which can be prevented by using SafeMath libraries or Solidity's built-in overflow protection mechanisms.

Front-running attacks occur when malicious actors manipulate pending transactions by adjusting gas fees to prioritize their trades, gaining an unfair advantage. This is particularly common in DeFi protocols. Developers can prevent front-running by implementing commit-reveal schemes, using private transaction pools, or utilizing batch processing techniques. Oracle manipulation is another major security risk, where attackers exploit price oracles to force artificial liquidations or manipulate lending and borrowing rates. Using decentralized oracles like Chainlink or Band Protocol, implementing time-weighted average pricing (TWAP), and setting up fallback mechanisms can reduce the risk of price manipulation.

Access control flaws are a major concern in smart contract security, where poorly implemented permissions allow unauthorized users to execute sensitive functions. Developers should use role-based access control (RBAC), multi-signature authentication, and time-locked administrative actions to prevent unauthorized changes. Additionally, ensuring that smart contract functions that modify critical parameters are restricted to trusted addresses or governance mechanisms enhances security.

Unit testing and formal verification are crucial for validating contract logic before deployment. Using frameworks like Hardhat, Truffle, and Foundry, developers can write comprehensive test cases covering normal operations, edge cases, and potential attack scenarios. Formal verification mathematically proves that a contract's execution aligns with its intended logic, reducing risks associated with unexpected behaviors.

Engaging with third-party security auditors provides an additional layer of protection. Professional audit firms such as CertiK, OpenZeppelin, Trail of Bits, and PeckShield conduct in-depth analysis, including manual code review, automated vulnerability scanning, and penetration testing. Audit reports help projects identify weaknesses, improve security measures, and reassure investors and users about the project's reliability.

Bug bounty programs incentivize ethical hackers to discover vulnerabilities before bad actors exploit them. Platforms like Immunefi and HackerOne allow developers to set rewards for responsibly disclosed security issues. By leveraging the expertise of the global security community, projects can identify and patch vulnerabilities before going live.

Secure deployment strategies ensure that the contract is launched safely and remains protected post-deployment. Developers should deploy contracts on testnets like Goerli, Sepolia, or Binance Smart Chain Testnet before mainnet migration. Verifying contract addresses, maintaining read-only function verifications, and monitoring transaction logs help prevent misconfigurations. If a contract needs upgradability, transparent proxy patterns, governance-controlled upgrades, and timelocks should be implemented to prevent unauthorized modifications.

Continuous monitoring and threat detection are essential post-deployment. Tools such as Forta, OpenZeppelin Defender, and Chainalysis help detect anomalies, suspicious transactions, and potential exploits. Smart contracts should also include emergency response mechanisms, such as circuit breakers, pause functions, and withdrawal limits, to mitigate damage in case of an exploit.

By following security best practices—including secure coding standards, rigorous auditing, continuous monitoring, and governance-controlled upgrades—projects can significantly reduce vulnerabilities and enhance the security of their smart contracts. Prioritizing security at every stage, from development to post-deployment, ensures a safer blockchain ecosystem, builds trust among users, and protects digital assets from malicious attacks.

Legal and Regulatory Compliance Across Different Jurisdictions

Legal and regulatory compliance across different jurisdictions is a crucial aspect of launching and managing a cryptocurrency project. As the global regulatory landscape evolves, crypto businesses must navigate complex frameworks that vary significantly between countries. Compliance with regulations related to securities laws, Know Your Customer (KYC), Anti-Money Laundering (AML), tax obligations, and data protection ensures long-term sustainability and prevents legal risks, including fines, delistings, and restrictions on operations.

In the United States, the regulatory environment is one of the most complex and stringent. The Securities and Exchange Commission (SEC) determines whether a token is classified as a security under the Howey Test, which assesses whether an investment involves an expectation of profit from the efforts of others.

If classified as a security, the token must comply with SEC registration and disclosure requirements unless exemptions apply. The Commodity Futures Trading Commission (CFTC) regulates crypto derivatives, while the Financial Crimes Enforcement Network (FinCEN) enforces AML requirements for exchanges and crypto service providers. State-level regulations, such as the New York BitLicense, impose additional compliance burdens.

In the European Union (EU), the Markets in Crypto-Assets (MiCA) regulation establishes a unified framework for crypto regulation across member states. MiCA introduces licensing requirements for crypto service providers, stablecoin issuers, and token projects while ensuring consumer protection and market integrity. The Fifth and Sixth Anti-Money Laundering Directives (AMLD5 & AMLD6) impose strict KYC and AML obligations on exchanges and custodial wallet providers. The General Data Protection Regulation (GDPR) applies to crypto businesses that process personal data, requiring strict data protection and consent mechanisms.

Switzerland has positioned itself as a crypto-friendly jurisdiction, with clear legal frameworks provided by FINMA (Swiss Financial Market Supervisory Authority). Crypto projects can be categorized as payment tokens, utility tokens, or asset tokens, each with specific regulatory requirements. Self-regulatory organizations (SROs) oversee compliance with AML rules, and blockchain startups often establish entities in Zug's Crypto Valley, benefiting from a favorable regulatory climate.

Singapore is another preferred jurisdiction for crypto businesses due to its progressive approach to blockchain innovation. The Monetary Authority of Singapore (MAS) regulates crypto under the

Payment Services Act (PSA), requiring licensing for exchanges and custodians. The city-state follows AML/CFT (Countering the Financing of Terrorism) compliance standards while fostering blockchain innovation through regulatory sandboxes.

Japan has one of the most structured regulatory environments, with the Financial Services Agency (FSA) overseeing crypto exchanges and service providers. The Payment Services Act classifies cryptocurrencies as digital assets and mandates strict AML/KYC compliance, exchange licensing, and security audits. The Japan Virtual Currency Exchange Association (JVCEA) plays a role in self-regulating the industry, ensuring that crypto businesses follow best practices.

Hong Kong has recently introduced a comprehensive crypto licensing framework, requiring virtual asset service providers (VASPs) to obtain licenses from the Securities and Futures Commission (SFC). Hong Kong remains open to crypto businesses, particularly those focused on institutional trading and tokenized securities.

The United Kingdom (UK) regulates crypto under Financial Conduct Authority (FCA) guidelines, with a strong focus on AML/KYC compliance and stablecoin oversight. While the UK does not impose blanket bans on crypto, projects must comply with crypto asset registration requirements, particularly those offering financial services or derivatives.

China has imposed strict bans on crypto trading, ICOs, and mining activities, enforcing regulatory crackdowns on digital assets. However, the country actively promotes blockchain innovation through its central bank digital currency (CBDC) initiative, the digital yuan (e-CNY).

India has had an uncertain regulatory stance, with fluctuating government policies regarding crypto taxation, exchange operations, and potential bans. In 2022, the government imposed a 30% tax on crypto profits and a 1% transaction tax (TDS) on crypto trades, signaling an intent to regulate rather than ban the industry entirely.

The Middle East, particularly the UAE (Dubai and Abu Dhabi), has emerged as a crypto-friendly region. The Dubai Virtual Assets Regulatory Authority (VARA) provides a regulatory framework for crypto businesses, exchanges, and security token offerings. Abu Dhabi's ADGM (Abu Dhabi Global Market) and FSRA (Financial Services Regulatory Authority) offer licensing options for digital asset firms.

Navigating legal compliance requires securing proper licenses, adhering to KYC/AML requirements, understanding token classifications, ensuring data protection compliance, and addressing tax obligations. Many crypto projects register in crypto-friendly jurisdictions like Switzerland, Singapore, the UAE, and the Cayman Islands to minimize regulatory burdens while maintaining legal credibility. Partnering with legal advisory firms, regulatory compliance consultants, and blockchain security firms ensures that a project meets all legal requirements while scaling operations globally. By staying compliant, crypto businesses can avoid legal pitfalls, gain investor confidence, and position themselves for long-term success in the evolving regulatory landscape.

Future-Proofing Your Cryptocurrency

Future-proofing a cryptocurrency project is essential for long-term sustainability, security, and adaptability in an ever-evolving blockchain ecosystem. Rapid advancements in blockchain technology, regulatory shifts, and changing market dynamics require proactive strategies to ensure continued relevance, adoption, and resilience against emerging risks. Projects that fail to anticipate future challenges may face obsolescence, security vulnerabilities, or regulatory restrictions, making future-proofing a key priority for blockchain developers, investors, and communities.

Ensuring scalability is a fundamental aspect of future-proofing a cryptocurrency. As blockchain networks grow, increased transaction volume can lead to congestion, high fees, and slower processing times. Implementing Layer-2 scaling solutions, such as Optimistic Rollups, ZK-Rollups, and state channels, can improve transaction speeds and reduce costs while maintaining decentralization. Sharding, used in networks like Ethereum 2.0 and Polkadot, enables parallel transaction processing, enhancing efficiency without overloading a single chain. Adopting an architecture that supports modular upgrades ensures that future scalability improvements can be integrated seamlessly.

Security remains a cornerstone of any long-term cryptocurrency strategy. As cyber threats evolve, robust security measures must be continuously updated. Regular smart contract audits, penetration testing, and formal verification minimize vulnerabilities. Using multi-signature wallets, time-locked transactions, and circuit breakers enhances security for treasury funds and protocol operations. Bug bounty programs incentivize ethical hackers to identify potential exploits before malicious actors can take advantage of them. Post-deployment, integrating real-time threat monitoring systems such as Forta and OpenZeppelin Defender enables proactive incident response.

Interoperability is critical for ensuring long-term adoption and integration within the broader blockchain ecosystem. Many cryptocurrencies operate in isolated ecosystems, limiting their utility. Supporting cross-chain compatibility through bridges, wrapped assets, and blockchain interoperability protocols like Cosmos IBC and Polkadot XCMP ensures that a cryptocurrency remains adaptable to new developments. Smart contract platforms that support multiple virtual machines (VMs), such as Ethereum's EVM and WASM-based environments, allow developers to deploy across different ecosystems without major modifications.

Regulatory adaptability is another key component of future-proofing. With governments worldwide imposing varying degrees of regulation, projects must be prepared for evolving legal requirements. Implementing compliance frameworks for KYC/AML, token classification, and financial reporting ensures that a cryptocurrency remains legally compliant while avoiding enforcement actions or delistings from exchanges. Registering in crypto-friendly jurisdictions such as Switzerland, Singapore, or the UAE allows projects to operate within a regulatory framework that balances innovation and compliance. Decentralized Autonomous Organization (DAO) governance models provide legal flexibility while maintaining community-driven decision-making.

Tokenomics optimization ensures long-term economic sustainability and prevents issues such as inflation, low utility, or liquidity crises. Designing dynamic supply mechanisms, staking incentives, and sustainable reward structures ensures that token distribution aligns with network growth. Implementing adaptive fee mechanisms, burning mechanisms, or token buybacks can help maintain scarcity and stabilize value. Liquidity provisioning strategies, including market-making partnerships, automated liquidity management, and incentivized liquidity mining, ensure that the cryptocurrency remains tradable across major exchanges.

Decentralized governance models enhance resilience by allowing the community to adapt protocols over time. DAOs, quadratic voting, and delegated governance models give stakeholders decision-making power, ensuring that the project evolves based on collective consensus. Implementing upgradable smart contracts with transparent voting mechanisms allows necessary improvements without compromising security. Ensuring that governance remains resistant to centralization and Sybil attacks safeguards the integrity of community-driven decision-making.

Sustainable energy practices and environmental considerations are increasingly important for the longevity of blockchain projects. Cryptocurrencies utilizing Proof of Stake (PoS) or hybrid consensus mechanisms significantly reduce energy consumption compared to Proof of Work (PoW) models. Blockchain networks that integrate carbon offset programs, green mining incentives, or renewable energy partnerships enhance their long-term viability while aligning with global sustainability goals.

User adoption and real-world utility ensure that a cryptocurrency remains relevant beyond speculative trading. Expanding merchant acceptance, DeFi integrations, enterprise partnerships, and NFT ecosystems strengthens real-world use cases. Supporting microtransactions, stablecoin integrations, and remittance solutions broadens the cryptocurrency's adoption across various industries. Continuous developer support, hackathons, grants, and open-source contributions foster innovation within the ecosystem, ensuring a steady flow of new applications built on the network.

Future-proofing a cryptocurrency requires scalability, security, interoperability, regulatory compliance, sustainable tokenomics, decentralized governance, environmental considerations, and real-world utility. By integrating these elements, projects can navigate market volatility, regulatory uncertainty, and technological advancements while maintaining long-term growth and adoption. Proactive development, security enhancements, and community-driven innovation will define the next generation of resilient and future-proofed cryptocurrencies.

Chapter 11
Scaling and Evolving Your Cryptocurrency

Scaling and evolving a cryptocurrency requires continuous innovation in scalability, security, interoperability, governance, and real-world adoption. Layer-2 solutions like rollups, sidechains, and state channels enhance transaction speed and reduce costs, ensuring network efficiency. Robust security measures, including audits, real-time monitoring, and multi-signature protections, prevent exploits and strengthen resilience.

Cross-chain interoperability expands utility through blockchain bridges and decentralized protocols like Cosmos IBC and Polkadot. Regulatory adaptability ensures compliance with evolving laws, integrating KYC/AML measures while maintaining decentralization via DAOs. Optimized tokenomics, including staking rewards, adaptive fees, and liquidity management, promote long-term sustainability and ecosystem stability.

Decentralized governance allows transparent, community-driven upgrades, ensuring protocol evolution aligns with user interests. Eco-friendly consensus models, such as Proof of Stake, enhance sustainability and regulatory favorability. Expanding real-world use cases in payments, DeFi, and NFTs drives mainstream adoption, while developer grants and partnerships fuel innovation. A future-proof cryptocurrency balances scalability, security, compliance, and utility to ensure long-term success in the evolving blockchain landscape.

Upgrading the Protocol and Implementing Hard Forks

Upgrading a cryptocurrency protocol and implementing hard forks are crucial for enhancing security, scalability, and functionality. As blockchain networks evolve, upgrades ensure efficiency, fix vulnerabilities, and introduce new features. These upgrades can be soft forks, which maintain backward compatibility, or hard forks, which create a new blockchain version that is incompatible with previous rules.

A hard fork occurs when significant protocol changes require all network participants—miners, validators, and node operators—to upgrade their software. If consensus is not reached, a split can occur, resulting in two separate chains, as seen with Bitcoin and Bitcoin Cash or Ethereum and Ethereum Classic. Hard forks can be planned, introducing upgrades like Ethereum's Merge, or contentious, where disagreements lead to a network split.

Successful protocol upgrades require community consensus, thorough testing, and transparent communication. Using testnets, developer audits, and multi-phase deployments ensures stability before launching on the mainnet. DAOs or governance models facilitate democratic decision-making, allowing token holders to vote on proposed changes.

Challenges in implementing hard forks include network fragmentation, user confusion, and exchange support. To mitigate risks, developers must provide clear upgrade instructions, ensure exchange compatibility, and educate the community about the benefits. Security concerns, such as replay attacks—where transactions on one chain are replicated on another—can be prevented through transaction differentiation mechanisms.

Upgrading a protocol strengthens a blockchain's long-term viability, improves performance, and enables innovation. Well-executed hard forks can enhance decentralization, scalability, and adoption while maintaining network integrity. Transparent governance, rigorous testing, and broad community participation are key to ensuring a smooth and effective upgrade process.

Cross-Chain Integrations and Interoperability

seamless exchange of assets and data across multiple blockchain networks. As the blockchain ecosystem expands, projects must ensure that their cryptocurrency can interact with different chains, reducing silos and increasing utility. Interoperability enhances liquidity, improves scalability, and enables decentralized applications (dApps) to leverage the strengths of multiple networks.

Blockchain interoperability is achieved through bridges, wrapped tokens, and cross-chain protocols. Bridges, such as Wormhole, Synapse, and Multichain, facilitate asset transfers between chains by locking tokens on one network and minting equivalent representations on another. Wrapped tokens, like Wrapped Bitcoin (WBTC), enable assets from one blockchain to function on another, increasing liquidity and expanding use cases. Cross-chain messaging protocols, such as Cosmos IBC (Inter-Blockchain Communication), Polkadot XCMP (Cross-Chain Message Passing), and Chainlink CCIP (Cross-Chain Interoperability Protocol), allow smart contracts and applications to communicate across blockchains.

Interoperability benefits DeFi, NFT ecosystems, and enterprise blockchain solutions by enabling cross-chain trading, liquidity pools, and decentralized identity verification. Projects integrating multiple networks increase accessibility, reduce dependency on a single blockchain, and attract a broader user base. Challenges include security risks, bridge exploits, and protocol incompatibilities, requiring audits, multi-signature protections, and decentralized bridge governance to minimize vulnerabilities.

A successful cross-chain integration strategy prioritizes security, user experience, and efficient transaction execution. As blockchain technology advances, interoperability will drive broader adoption, ensuring that cryptocurrencies can function seamlessly across ecosystems. By embracing multi-chain compatibility, projects position themselves for sustained growth and relevance in an interconnected blockchain future.

Staking and Yield Farming for Token Holders

Staking and yield farming provide token holders with opportunities to earn passive income while contributing to the security and liquidity of a blockchain network. These mechanisms incentivize long-term participation, enhance token utility, and support decentralized finance (DeFi) ecosystems.

Staking involves locking tokens in a blockchain network to support consensus mechanisms like Proof of Stake (PoS) or Delegated Proof of Stake (DPoS). In return, stakers receive rewards in the form of additional tokens. PoS networks, such as Ethereum 2.0, Cardano, and Polkadot, use staking to validate transactions and secure the network. Token holders can stake individually, delegate their stake to validators, or participate in staking pools to maximize rewards. Factors such as staking duration, slashing penalties, and network inflation rates impact reward structures.

Yield farming allows users to earn rewards by providing liquidity to decentralized exchanges (DEXs) and lending protocols. Participants deposit tokens into liquidity pools on platforms like Uniswap, SushiSwap, and PancakeSwap, earning transaction fees and governance tokens as rewards. Strategies such as liquidity mining, auto-compounding, and dual-yield farming optimize returns but come with risks, including impermanent loss, smart contract vulnerabilities, and market volatility.

Both staking and yield farming incentivize long-term token holding, reducing sell pressure while rewarding users for supporting the network. Security considerations, including audited smart contracts, multi-signature withdrawals, and decentralized governance, are essential to mitigate risks. By integrating staking and yield farming, projects create sustainable economic incentives, ensuring token stability, liquidity, and community engagement.

Long-Term Sustainability and Growth Strategies

Long-term sustainability and growth strategies are essential for ensuring the continued success, adoption, and resilience of a cryptocurrency project. As the blockchain industry evolves, projects must implement robust mechanisms that foster ecosystem stability, incentivize participation, and adapt to regulatory and technological changes.

A well-structured tokenomics model is crucial for long-term sustainability. Implementing balanced supply mechanisms, staking incentives, deflationary strategies, and liquidity management ensures that token distribution aligns with network growth. Mechanisms such as gradual vesting, token burns, and adaptive fees prevent inflation and maintain scarcity while encouraging long-term holding.

Decentralized governance structures, including DAOs (Decentralized Autonomous Organizations) and on-chain voting, empower the community to guide protocol upgrades and resource allocation. Transparent governance fosters trust, enhances decentralization, and ensures that decisions reflect the interests of token holders. Multi-signature treasury management and periodic governance audits further strengthen credibility.

Continuous technical innovation and scalability solutions are essential for sustaining network efficiency. Adopting Layer-2 scaling solutions, interoperability protocols, and modular smart contract upgrades ensures that the network remains competitive. Supporting multi-chain deployments and cross-chain integrations expands the project's ecosystem, increasing accessibility and adoption.

Security and compliance must remain a priority to protect the network and users. Regular smart contract audits, bug bounty programs, and real-time monitoring mitigate vulnerabilities, while adherence to KYC/AML regulations and evolving global policies prevents legal risks. Establishing compliance partnerships and obtaining necessary licenses in crypto-friendly jurisdictions strengthens regulatory resilience.

Community engagement and ecosystem growth drive long-term adoption. Incentivizing developer participation through grants, hackathons, and open-source contributions fosters innovation. Expanding real-world utility by integrating with DeFi platforms, NFT ecosystems, enterprise solutions, and payment networks ensures sustained demand. Marketing efforts, including strategic partnerships, influencer collaborations, and educational content, enhance visibility and user retention.

A strong sustainability strategy balances tokenomics, governance, technical innovation, security, compliance, and ecosystem growth. By continuously evolving, engaging the community, and staying adaptable to industry trends, a cryptocurrency project can achieve long-term success and resilience in the ever-changing blockchain landscape.

Conclusion

The journey of creating and sustaining a cryptocurrency requires a deep understanding of blockchain technology, security, governance, and market dynamics. From conceptualizing a token to ensuring its long-term adoption, successful projects navigate challenges through innovation, adaptability, and community-driven development. As the crypto space evolves, lessons from established cryptocurrencies, the future of decentralized finance (DeFi), overcoming industry challenges, and the roadmap to mainstream adoption serve as guiding principles for any new project.

Leading cryptocurrencies like Bitcoin, Ethereum, and Binance Smart Chain have demonstrated key strategies for long-term success. Bitcoin pioneered decentralized finance by proving the resilience of blockchain as a trustless network. Ethereum introduced smart contracts and dApp ecosystems, enabling a new wave of DeFi, NFTs, and tokenization. Binance Smart Chain capitalized on low-cost, high-speed transactions, ensuring mass adoption. These projects emphasize security, network decentralization, developer engagement, and regulatory adaptability as pillars of sustainability. Learning from their growth, new projects must prioritize a scalable infrastructure, clear tokenomics, and a committed user base to achieve long-term viability.

DeFi has transformed traditional finance by enabling permissionless lending, staking, and liquidity farming. The next phase of DeFi will focus on cross-chain integrations, real-world asset tokenization, and institutional adoption. Scalable solutions like

Layer-2 rollups and cross-chain interoperability protocols will eliminate bottlenecks, ensuring seamless financial operations. Decentralized autonomous organizations (DAOs) will redefine governance, giving users more control over financial ecosystems. The convergence of DeFi with AI, GameFi, and decentralized identity will further accelerate innovation, making blockchain finance more inclusive and secure.

Despite its rapid growth, the crypto industry faces regulatory uncertainty, scalability limitations, security vulnerabilities, and public skepticism. Governments worldwide continue to impose regulatory frameworks, requiring projects to ensure KYC/AML compliance, legal transparency, and responsible financial management. Scalability remains an ongoing challenge, pushing networks to adopt Layer-2 scaling, sharding, and efficient consensus mechanisms to handle mass transactions. Security concerns, including hacks, smart contract exploits, and bridge vulnerabilities, demand regular audits, bug bounties, and decentralized governance for risk mitigation. Public trust remains a barrier, requiring education, real-world adoption, and transparent communication to foster legitimacy.

For a cryptocurrency to move from concept to mainstream adoption, it must address usability, security, scalability, and regulatory integration. Building an engaged community through transparent governance, staking incentives, and ecosystem rewards strengthens adoption. Listing on centralized and decentralized exchanges, integrating with DeFi protocols, NFT marketplaces, and fintech solutions, and forming institutional partnerships increase utility and accessibility. Bridging gaps between traditional finance and blockchain through merchant payments, stablecoin integrations, and real-world applications will further drive adoption.

The future of cryptocurrency lies in innovation, decentralization, and community trust. By learning from successful projects, adapting to DeFi advancements, overcoming industry challenges, and focusing on mainstream adoption strategies, any cryptocurrency can achieve long-term sustainability. As blockchain technology continues to evolve, the pioneers of tomorrow will be those who prioritize security, governance, and real-world utility, ensuring that their projects withstand the test of time and shape the future of decentralized finance.

www.ingramcontent.com/pod-product-compliance
Lightning Source LLC
Chambersburg PA
CBHW041300210926
51847CB00009B/81
9789696592648